Winning Westminster

How Labour turned Westminster Council Red

Paul Dimoldenberg

Contents

Foreword

The Westminster Labour Team

Bibliography

About the Author

"I am a great believer in luck, and I find the harder I work, the more I have of it."

Thomas Jefferson, third President of the United States (1801–1809)

"The most expensive property on the Monopoly board is Mayfair, which also happens to be the most exclusive expanse of real estate in real-life London. Flush with private equity firms, eye-wateringly expensive restaurants and luxury car showrooms, it voted Labour in last week's local elections and helped swing Westminster council away from the Tories for the first time since the Beatles were in the charts with Can't Buy Me Love."

Andrew Anthony, '*UK local elections: how London turned from blue to red*', The Observer, 8th May 2022

"It's amazing what you can accomplish when you do not care who gets the credit."

Harry S. Truman, 33rd president of the United States (1945-1953)

Foreword

Winning Westminster City Council for the Labour Party had been a long-held, but unfulfilled, ambition. Until 5th May 2022.

It has been a long march, with many twists and turns, highs and lows, occasional successes and countless failures. Karen Buck, MP for Westminster North, and I would regularly share Samuel Beckett's never-give-up advice, usually after the latest Council election defeat, *"Ever tried. Ever failed. No matter. Try again. Fail again. Fail better."* We would then promise to 'redouble' our efforts, again.

Many people do not realise that Westminster is a city of two halves, a place where the rich and poor live 'cheek by jowl'. Westminster includes all the top tourist spots - Buckingham Palace, Westminster Abbey, Whitehall, 10 Downing Street, Covent Garden, The Royal Parks and Trafalgar Square. The affluent 'Monopoly-board' areas are well known, too – Mayfair, Park Lane, Knightsbridge, Belgravia, St John's Wood and Marylebone – where those working in Westminster's successful professional, finance and property industries live.

But there are areas of deprivation close by in north Paddington, Church Street, Soho and Pimlico to rival anywhere in the UK, as the following facts and figures reveal:

- In 2019/20, 36% of people in Westminster lived in households with an income of less than 60% the UK median after housing costs have been subtracted.
- 25% of children in Westminster lived in households with an income of less than 60% the UK median after housing costs have been subtracted in 2020/21.
- 14.2% of Westminster residents were estimated to be earning below the Living Wage in 2021.

- Youth Unemployment rates vary from less than 1% in more affluent wards up to 16% in more deprived areas, such as Church Street.
- Life expectancy is 13.5 years lower for men and 7.4 years lower for women in the most deprived areas of Westminster than in the least deprived areas.

Westminster is also a very diverse, multi-cultural city with over 88 nationalities and 85 languages spoken in addition to English. According to the 2021 census, the population in Westminster is predominantly white (55.2%), with non-white minorities representing the remaining 44.8% of the population. Asian people are the largest minority group in Westminster, accounting for 16.8% of the population, with Black people making up 8% of the Westminster population.

We were close to winning the Council in 1986, when Labour won 27 Labour Councillors to the Conservatives' 32 Councillors. Every vote at Council meetings was close for the next four years, Our Chief Whip, Andrew Dismore was a master of Standing Orders and he would regularly try to catch out the Conservatives by interrupting Council proceedings with a Point of Order, invoking a sub-clause of an obscure Standing Order. *"We've got'em now!"* he would shout, *"just where want them."* Only for the City Solicitor to advise the Lord Mayor that the sub-clause Andrew cited was not applicable in this case.

But in May 2022, Labour did not have to rely on Points of Order or Standing Orders to win control of Westminster City Council. At this election all the stars aligned in the same direction – an unpopular Conservative Government, a law-breaking Prime Minister, an arrogant and complacent local Council responsible for spectacular financial blunders and, of course, a positive Labour alternative plan – to bring about a Labour victory.

Few, if any of Labour's successful candidates expected to win the Council. Some, like me, were even surprised to win their

Ward. But it was not a fluke. It was the result of many years' campaigning and representing the concerns and interests of local residents.

Many people were involved in Labour's historic Westminster win, all of whom deserve credit and thanks for their contributions over many years. So many clever and talented people have passed through Westminster Labour Party. Some were born here, others made the area their long-term home, while for many it was a 'staging post' on a path to other parts of London and beyond. I have been fortunate to have made some life-long friends.

Thankfully, we have avoided the worst of the destructive and pointless infighting that has bedevilled some of our Labour neighbours. Fighting the hard-hearted Westminster Conservatives has always been a much better use of our time. It brought people together in a common endeavour and created a camaraderie and a positive approach to our politics. With no fear of failure and a 'glass half full' attitude, we have always seen the upside of any change or new opportunity.

As a Labour Opposition Councillor for over 30 years with little, if any, prospect of winning the Council, people often used to ask me, "why do you still do it?" The answer I always gave was this, *"There are around 30-40% of Westminster residents who vote Labour and they deserve effective representation no matter who runs the Council."* The fact that there has been a permanent Conservative majority on Westminster City Council since 1964 means that Labour voters have needed effective representation even more!

I have long learned that you have to play whatever hand you are dealt; your duty is to do the very best you can to represent the people who elected you. The job is to "get things done". Sometimes, with that comes political power; other times, as in my 30-odd years in Opposition in Westminster, you just have to be satisfied with doing a good job for your constituents.

And sometimes, when you are least expecting it, the impossible happens. Others will no doubt have their own stories to tell, but this is my personal 'inside story' of how Labour turned Westminster City Council red - when a new door opened and we started to deliver a Fairer Westminster.

I hope you enjoy it; I certainly enjoyed writing it!

Paul Dimoldenberg,
April   2023

The Westminster Labour Team

Winning Westminster was a team effort involving Councillors in the Labour Group, Council candidates, constituency officers from Westminster North and Cities of London & Westminster Labour Parties, Karen Buck MP and individual Labour Party members and volunteers. Everyone played their part and together we pulled off a remarkable victory.

The Westminster Labour Team was full of exceptional people from diverse backgrounds, experiences and 'back-stories'. Some had long experience of opposition in local government, while others had no experience of life on their local council. Our Team included people from their early-twenties to their mid-seventies. A multi-ethnic group, we included black, brown and white people. There were Christians, Jews, Muslims and those of other faiths and none. Our numbers included straight and gay people, with some mums and dads and a few grandparents.

Some were born and bred in Westminster, while others came from all over the UK and from across the globe to make their home in Westminster. Our Team included those working in the public, private, voluntary and community sectors, and others with experience in the arts, culture, sport, the law, trade unions, health and education. We included people with business skills and those who had run national and international organisations. Together, our experience stretched from the shop floor to the board room.

We were a remarkably cohesive and interesting group of people, reflecting the multi-cultural Westminster we lived in – 'a team of many talents'.

The Councillors and Member of Parliament

Adam Hug, Leader of the Westminster Labour Group, was elected a Councillor for Westbourne Ward in 2010. Originally from Portsmouth, he was Director of the Foreign Policy Centre from 2017 to 2022. He had previously been the Policy Director at the Foreign Policy Centre from 2008-2017. His research focused on human rights and governance (particularly in the former Soviet Union), UK foreign policy and EU issues.

Karen Buck, Member of Parliament for Westminster North, was first elected for Regent's Park and Kensington North in 1997. When the boundaries changed in 2010, she was elected Member of Parliament for Westminster North. She is currently Shadow Minister for Social Security. Karen Buck's Private Member's Bill received Royal Assent as the Homes (Fitness for Human Habitation) Act, 2018. Tenants can now take landlords to court if they fail to let or maintain property in a condition that is fit for human habitation. She was a Councillor for Queen's Park Ward from 1990-1997.

Aicha Less was born in Morocco and went to school in Westminster. She was elected a Councillor for the Church Street Ward in 2016, the first Moroccan to win a seat in British local elections. She is Deputy Leader of the Labour Group and is a governor at the Portman Centre for Families and Children. Aicha worked as political officer for the Local Government Association Labour Group.

Tim Roca has been a Councillor for the Harrow Road Ward since 2015 and is Deputy Leader of the Labour Group. Originally from the Northwest, he works in higher education at a London University. He was the Labour Candidate for Macclesfield at the 2015 General Election.

Geoff Barraclough has been a Maida Vale Ward Councillor since 2018 and has lived in Maida Vale for over twenty years. Geoff worked in business for an international technology company and has a degree in Economics.

Councillor Liza Begum was born and raised in Pimlico and was first elected as a Churchill Ward Councillor at a by-election in 2021. Prior to her election, she led a successful campaign to stop the redevelopment of the council estate she grew up in, resulting in residents being offered a right of return. Her working career has been in the public sector, in the NHS and more recently as a Training and Engagement Officer at a local Westminster charity, helping women get back into work.

David Boothroyd has represented Westbourne Ward since 2002. From Yorkshire, he grew up in Cheshire and after graduating from Cambridge University has worked as a researcher for Members of Parliament and in the private sector, He is the author of *'Politico's guide to the history of British political parties'*, which describes every political party which has fought a Westminster general election or by-election since 1832.

Ruth Bush was first elected to represent the Harrow Road Ward in 2005. With strong links to the local community, Ruth ran a hostel for young homeless women, worked as a secretary at the House of Commons and was Age Concern's Parliamentary Officer. In 2019-20, Ruth was the first ever Labour Lord Mayor of Westminster.

Nafsika Butler-Thalasis has been a Maida Vale Ward Councillor since 2018. She is an EU citizen who came to the UK from Greece as a child and chose to make Britain her home. She has lived in Maida Vale for 23 years and has a PhD in the history of British military psychiatry. Nafsika is CEO of a local health charity.

Maggie Carman was first elected as a Bayswater Ward Councillor in 2018 and has worked tirelessly for residents ever since, from getting families out of bad housing to stopping the development of a coach station at Royal Oak as a replacement for Victoria coach station. Originally from south London she was an English lecturer before she retired.

Paul Dimoldenberg was first elected as a Harrow Road Ward Councillor from 1982 – 1990 and in 1997, he was elected as a Queen's Park Ward Councillor. A former Leader of the Labour Group, he led the Team that uncovered the 'Homes for Votes' and '15p Cemeteries' scandals. Originally from Manchester, in 2022, he decided to step down from Queen's Park Ward and run in the Conservative-held Hyde Park Ward. He is chair of a public relations company he co-founded.

Pancho Lewis was the first Labour Councillor elected for the West End Ward in 2018. A passionate environmentalist, he has worked as a parliamentary researcher and for a number of social enterprises. He stood down from the Council in 2022 to pursue an academic career.

Patricia McAllister was elected as a Queen's Park Ward Councillor in 2009. Originally from Scotland, Patricia has been involved with a Special Needs Group for over 20 years. She helps with collections for the North Paddington Food Bank. Patricia worked for the DWP for 30 years.

Matt Noble was first elected as a Church Street Ward Councillor in 2018. Originally from Huddersfield, he works for a software company, having previously been involved in the property industry.

Hamza Taouzzale, was first elected to represent Queen's Park Ward in 2018. At 18 years of age, he was the youngest member of the Council. He holds a Masters' degree in global affairs from King's College London. He previously represented Westminster's young people as a Member of the Youth Parliament. Of Moroccan heritage, he was born and bred on the Lisson Green Estate. He has also appeared in a Stormzy video.

Aziz Toki has been Councillor for Church Street Ward since 2006. He runs the Central London Youth Development Trust, based in Penfold Street, which during lockdown helped to feed more than 100 families, and provided activity packs and cooking lessons to vulnerable children in the north of Westminster. He has a BA degree from Chittagong University, Bangladesh.

Rita Begum served as a Maida Vale Ward Councillor from 2014-2022. She went to school in Paddington and worked for a number of local charities. She was the Labour candidate for the West Central division at the London Assembly elections in 2021. She stood down in 2022 as she had moved to Brent and was subsequently elected as a Brent Councillor.

Guthrie McKie was elected as a Harrow Road Councillor in 2000. Born in Scotland, Guthrie is a former Trade Union Organiser in the paper and print industries. He stood down at the 2022 Council elections.

Papya Qureshi was first elected as a Councillor for Westbourne Ward in 2006 and served until 2022. Born and raised in Westminster, she worked as a primary school teacher before moving into the technology sector. She stood down at the 2022 Council elections.

Shamim Talukder was a Churchill Ward Councillor from 2014-2022 when he stood down. A film maker by profession, he was Development Officer for the Bengali Cultural Association.

Andrea Mann, originally from Wolverhampton and a screen writer, was elected as a Churchill Ward Councillor in 2018 and stood down for personal reasons, primarily, family care responsibilities, in 2021.

The Candidates

Concia Albert, a Harrow Road Ward Councillor, Concia has a wealth of experience in the voluntary and community sector in

Westminster and has worked in the as a volunteer and employee for 15 years. Concia has a degree in Social Policy with Sociology. She works in the NHS addressing health inequalities and was previously Head of Social Prescribing at voluntary sector organisation One Westminster.

Gillian Arrindell, a Vincent Square Ward Candidate, is an experienced adviser on Housing Rights, Homelessness, Welfare Benefits, Disability Rights, Debt Management, Employment Rights and Student Advice. She has an MA in Political Economy from the University of East London. A 1975 photograph by Harry Diamond of Gillian with her brothers is in the National Portrait Gallery collection. She stood unsuccessfully for election in the Tachbrook Ward in 2018.

Md Shamsed Chowdhury, a Hyde Park Ward candidate, has lived and worked in Westminster since 2016. He is experienced in the business and hospitality industries and keen to use his knowledge to support young people into work. Shamsed is also a volunteer with a homeless charity in Westminster.

Robert Eagleton, a Pimlico South Candidate, is from Preston, Lancashire and works for the DWP as a Senior Policy Adviser, previously having worked at DEFRA. A graduate of Birmingham University, he is a National Executive Member of the Public and Commercial Services Union.

Paul Fisher, a West End Ward Candidate, is originally from Cardiff, South Wales. A barrister by profession, he has a particular focus on complex construction, international arbitration and professional liability. He is a former trustee of the Covent Garden Area Trust.

Dario Goodwin, a Lancaster Gate Ward candidate, was also Campaign Organiser for the Westminster Labour election campaign. Previously a freelance editor, writer and researcher, he has worked with UN bodies, UK and European

Parliaments, and specialise in presenting complex information clearly.

Sara Hassan, a Little Venice Ward Candidate, is an experienced Middle East conflict and diplomacy specialist and is the Executive Director at Strategies for Peace. She previously managed the Middle East programme at the Oxford Research Group and spent time as a mediation adviser on Syria and Yemen. Sara trained as a journalist with Reuters and is fluent in Arabic. She has an MA in Conflict, Security and Development from the Department of War Studies, King's College London.

Ryan Jude, a Lancaster Gate Ward candidate, is a green finance expert. Originally from Stockport, he works for the Green Finance Institute, bringing together key stakeholders across the public and private sectors, academia and civil society in order to unlock barriers to the deployment of capital to deliver tangible economic outcomes.

Iman Less, a Maida Vale Ward Candidate, was born and raised in Westminster and has a Master's degree in economics and political science. She is the daughter of Councillor Aicha Less and stood for election unsuccessfully for the Little Venice Ward in 2018.

Patrick Lilley, a West End Ward Candidate, stood unsuccessfully for the West End Ward in 2018, losing by just 26 votes. Originally from Birmingham, he is a prominent LGBTQ activist and events promoter.

Ellie Ormsby, a Lancaster Gate Ward candidate, has helped neighbours sort problems on their streets and campaigned for a cleaner, greener and safer ward. Originally from Tameside in Greater Manchester, Ellie is a graduate of Oxford University and is a Senior Consultant for a major professional services firm.

David Parton, a Vincent Square Ward Candidate, is originally from Shropshire. He met fellow candidate Ellie Ormsby at university, where they co-chaired the university Labour club and became involved in Westminster Labour. David is a Senior Account Manager at a major public affairs consultancy, where he specialises in financial services. After the elections, David became Chair of Westminster North Labour Party.

Ananthi Paskaralingham, a Vincent Square Ward Candidate, stood unsuccessfully for the Vincent Square Ward in 2018.

Angela Piddock, a Westbourne Ward Candidate, was a Headteacher at a North Paddington primary school before she retired. She is a trustee and governor of several local organisations and schools. She was an unsuccessful candidate for Lancaster Gate Ward in 2018 and at a subsequent by-election. She is a former Chair of Westminster North Labour Party.

Murad Qureshi, a Little Venice Ward Candidate, was a councillor for Church Street Ward from 1998 to 2006 and was elected on the Labour Party's party list to the London Assembly from 2004–2016 and 2020-21. He stood unsuccessfully for the Little Venice Ward in 2018.

Cara Sanquest, a Queen's Park Ward Candidate, works for a charity and has previously worked in Parliament and for a range of social justice organisations. She has campaigned successfully on housing for victims of child criminal exploitation, hate crime reform, reproductive rights, child poverty and youth participation, and has been a trustee of Refugee Rights Europe.

James Small-Edwards was born and bred in Paddington. He has worked at a local food bank and was a vaccine marshal during the pandemic. A Candidate for Bayswater Ward, he read politics at Edinburgh then gained a Masters' degree at Oxford. He worked in Parliament as a researcher, was a scrum half in Wasps' academy and is the son of Heather

Small, singer with the band M People, and Shaun Edwards, who played rugby league for Wigan Warriors and is now coach to the French national rugby union team.

Judith Southern, a Hyde Park Ward candidate, grew up in rural Cumbria and trained to be a nursery nurse. She then worked in West Yorkshire as a bus driver before starting nurse training. She worked at Paddington Green Children's Hospital and has lived in Hyde Park ward since 1985. Before retiring she worked at Trinity Hospice at Clapham Common.

Max Sullivan, a Bayswater Ward candidate, has lived in the area since 2013. He was unsuccessful at the 2018 election when he ran as a candidate in Bayswater Ward. Originally from Ireland, he is an Account Director for a Paddington-based advertising agency and a former Chair of Westminster North Labour Party.

Jessica Toale, a West End Candidate, lives in Covent Garden. Jessica was the Centre for Development Results' first Executive Director. She has lectured on human rights, disaster risk reduction and community participation. Jessica has also written on foreign affairs, international development and cross-government working for the Fabian Society, the Guardian and the New Internationalist. She has an MSc in Urbanisation and Development from the London School of Economics and is a qualified barrister.

Jason Williams, a Pimlico South Candidate, was elected as a Churchill Ward Councillor in 2014 and was narrowly defeated by just 9 votes in 2018. Originally from North Wales, he works as a web editor with an international accountancy firm.

Rosie Wrighting, a Little Venice Candidate, is originally from North Northamptonshire. She works in the creative industries, for a global fashion retailer. In the pandemic she worked at a Community Hospital and volunteered in the community.

The Party Organisers

Margaret Lynch has been a stalwart of Westminster Labour Party since the 1980s and has served as Constituency Secretary and Election Organiser through countless campaigns. She was also Compliance Manager for the Labour Party until her retirement. Paddington born and bred, her parents moved to England from Ireland during the Blitz in search of work. Her younger brother, Michael, is General Secretary of the RMT trade union.

Andy Whitley has been Karen Buck's Election Agent and Treasurer of the Westminster North Labour Party for many years. Originally from Yorkshire, he was a Westbourne Ward Councillor from 1997-2002 and was Finance Spokesperson for the Labour Group.

Jacqueline Bore is the Election Agent for the Cities of London and Westminster. A senior lawyer with an international law firm, she specialises in the life sciences sector.

Connor Jones was Secretary of Westminster North Labour Party and was agent for the Lancaster Gate Ward candidates. Connor, who works in market research, organised focus groups to test and trial our campaign messages.

Chapter One – Stepping Down

I woke up on the morning of 3rd March 2021, my seventy-first birthday, with a weight off my mind. For the past week or so, I had been wrestling with thoughts about my future in local politics. I had been a Westminster City Councillor for over 32 years, all of it as a member of the Labour Opposition, and with the selection of candidates for the May 2022 Council elections about to start, I had to decide whether I wanted to continue to be a Labour Opposition Councillor for another four years. This would take me to the ripe old age of seventy-six. With some very good young candidates putting themselves forward for my Queen's Park Ward, it made good sense to step down and let a new generation continue to take on the fight with the Conservatives who had ruled Westminster Council ever since 1964.

While my decision to stand down was the right thing to do, after over 30 years on the Council, including fourteen years as Leader of the Opposition, it was not an easy one to take. First elected in 1982, I had been through some exciting and scary times, as I wrote in *'The Westminster Whistleblowers'*, which told the story of Dame Shirley Porter and the 'Homes for Votes' and 15p Cemeteries scandals and more. The Council was an important part of my life. Giving it up was a big decision.

So, how would I fill the 'gaping hole' in my life? In my mind, was my 'pandemic' experience which had given me the time to finish a book on the 1945 General Election which I had started writing twenty-five years earlier. From March to May 2020, I wrote *'Cheer Churchill. Vote Labour: The story of the 1945 General Election'*. I really enjoyed the experience, including self-publishing on Amazon. I followed this up in November 2020 with *'Building the New Jerusalem: How Attlee's Government built one million new homes'*. At the end of 2020, I started writing a life of London's Education pioneer, Sir Ashley Bramall, called *"A Sense of Duty'*, which I finished in

July 2021. I could see myself spending a lot more time researching and writing further books on Labour history. I was thinking that my next book would be about the birth of the NHS in 1948, another triumph of the post-war Attlee Government.

And another 'pandemic' experience was travelling around England (when we were allowed to do so!), visiting places my wife Linda and I had previously never been. We discovered Dorset, rediscovered the Northumberland coast and parts of the North-West and Yorkshire that previously had been just places on a map. The prospect of time for further road trips and train journeys to new places in the UK was very appealing. There was a lot of life to look forward to after May 2022. So, when I told Linda of my decision to step down from the Council she happily agreed.

After breakfast, and opening birthday presents, I started making calls. The first person I called was Margaret Lynch, a long-time friend, a former Labour Party senior official and the current Secretary of the Westminster Local Government Committee in charge of the local Council candidate selection process. Margaret had been a key driver of the Westminster Labour Party 'machine' for many decades – as Election Agent and Secretary for Westminster North MP Karen Buck, as well as a former Constituency Party Secretary and Organiser. I told her that another four years in Opposition was not something I was looking forward to and it would be better if Queen's Park Labour Party members selected someone else who really wanted to do the job. We discussed the prospects of winning the Council in 2022 and both agreed that the 2019 Local Government Boundary Commission decision to redraw the Westminster ward boundaries had not been kind to Labour. Winning the Council was not a realistic prospect.

I then called Labour Group Leader, Adam Hug, and my two fellow Queen's Park Ward Councillors, Patricia McAllister and Hamza Taouzzale, all of whom expressed surprise and disappointment but, after over 30 years, understood the reasons for my decision.

And, of course, I reassured them all that, for the next 14 months until May 2022, I would remain in top gear, giving everything to the Labour Group's efforts on the Council and in the forthcoming local election battles. But not, as it turned out, in the way they or I expected………

****

A week after I decided to step down at the May 2022 Council elections, Margaret Lynch called me. *"Have you thought about running in a Tory Ward?"* she asked. *"I have been walking around the new Knightsbridge & Belgravia ward,"* she said, *"and it now includes lots of Peabody blocks along Peabody Avenue that were previously in the former Churchill Ward. We have got previous canvass records and it looks a good base on which to mount a campaign."* Margaret argued, *"if we run a campaign in Knightsbridge & Belgravia we could divert some of the Tory efforts from our target ward, the new Pimlico South ward, which we know is going to be tough."*

The prospect of fighting the Tory stronghold of Knightsbridge & Belgravia did not interest me at all. It was not a part of Westminster that I was very familiar with and was some distance from where we lived on Marylebone Road. I told Margaret of my reluctance, but she wouldn't take no for answer. On 10th March she emailed me with a link to the Boundary Commission website, *"Hi Paul, You can look at the new ward boundaries here. Just in case you want to look at Knightsbridge."*

I was certainly attracted to the idea of running in a Conservative Ward to encourage the Tories into committing resources and people into fighting a ward they would normally do little other than deliver one election leaflet. If Knightsbridge & Belgravia was a 'Ward too far', then which Wards would I consider? I replied to Margaret, *"I was thinking more of*

Marylebone - I know it is impossible, but it is a lot more convenient and I already have a lot of contacts." Just across the road from where we live, Marylebone Ward included part of the Fitzrovia area where I had run unsuccessfully in 1990 and 1994 in the old Cavendish Ward, previously the most marginal Ward in Westminster.

The problem with the new Marylebone Ward was that the boundary changes had turned it into one of the strongest Conservative Wards. Margaret was not impressed by my suggestion and replied, *"I think Hyde Park is worth a go. We've haven't worked it since the HP by-election in 2012."* The boundary changes for Hyde Park Ward were a lot more interesting, with a large Conservative-voting area around Westbourne Terrace transferring into the Lancaster Gate Ward and a very mixed area of mansion blocks opposite Edgware Road underground station on Chapel Street, moving from Bryanston and Dorset Square Ward into Hyde Park Ward. Overall, according to figures extrapolated by our 'election guru' Councillor David Boothroyd, Hyde Park Ward would become the smallest ward in Westminster, with around 6,000 voters and a small notional increase in Labour voters. Before getting carried away, David's calculations estimated that the Conservatives would still get over 51% of the vote, based on the 2018 results, with Labour estimated to get 34.2% of the votes and the Lib Dems 9.8%.

In terms of convenience, the Hyde Park Ward could not have been better for me. I could see a lot of the Ward from the front room of our flat – the Edwardian mansion blocks on Old Marylebone Road, the 1960s Water Gardens apartments on Edgware Road and the new Paddington Basin development between Harrow Road and Praed Street. I would be a local candidate in every sense. I could contribute to the 2022 campaign, have some fun and with no pressure or expectation to win.

I was also very much attracted to being involved in a 'decoy campaign'. An avid reader of Ben McIntyre's books on Second

World War 'special operations', I liked the idea of running our very own version of 'Operation Fortitude'. Operation Fortitude was the code name for the Allies' World War II deception strategy in the run-up to the 1944 Normandy landings, with the aim of misleading the Nazis as to the location of the invasion. Our 'decoy operation' would have a twist. Whereas the Operation Fortitude plans involved the creation of a 'phantom' army in the Dover area to trick the Nazis into thinking that the invasion would come via the Pas de Calais, our 'Operation Hyde Park' would involve a real election campaign to divert Conservative resources from the marginal West End Ward. I replied back to Margaret, *"Yes, I think I will look at this seriously."*

Keen to test my idea, the following day, 11th March, I wrote to Patrick Lilley, Secretary of the Hyde Park Labour Branch and someone with whom I had worked closely on the West End Ward campaign from 2016-18. *"Is there any leaflet delivery to be done in Hyde Park Ward for the Mayoral elections?"* I asked. *"If so, please let me know and I am happy to do some."* In my mind, I had made my decision and 'Operation Hyde Park' was up and running.

Over the next few days, I picked up bundles of Sadiq Khan Mayoral election leaflets from the Westminster North office in Shirland Mews and started delivering them in parts of Hyde Park Ward where I knew there would be Labour supporters. I then wrote to Patrick again on 21st March,

"Just for your information, I am very interested in standing in Hyde Park Ward in 2022. I have been doing some Sadiq leaflet delivery in the Star Street/St Michael Street area and will be doing some more delivery this week. There are lots of front doors to put leaflets through so I would like to give the Tories a hard time over the next 12 months. It might divert some of them from attacking you in the West End.

Who should I talk to? I know Judith ran last time and might be interested in running again. Also, there are new voters in the

Basin area including all those affected by the cladding scandal."

Patrick replied the next day, *"Hi Paul, Judith really wants to stand and I got a leaflet from you so let's talk. There's maybe one or two other locals who might make a team."*

My response was rapid. *"That's great. Perhaps you, me and Judith should meet up? Just delivered over 300 leaflets at Dudley House and Paddington Gardens (both have letter boxes on the ground floor) and lots more at mews and street properties."*

The three of us agreed meet up in Norfolk Square, socially distanced, on Saturday 27th March. This was our first 'campaign meeting'.

I didn't know Judith Southern very well. She had been one of the three Labour Candidates for Hyde Park Ward who lost to the Conservatives in 2018. Judith had received 654 votes compared to the three winning Conservatives who all received around 1,100 votes each. Judith's running mates, Barbara Hainsworth and David Lumby received 674 and 598 respectively. Although Barbara and David were very much 'paper candidates', making up the numbers, Judith had put effort into the campaign, knocking on doors and talking to voters. She followed this up the following year during the 2019 General Election campaign, helped by a young supporter, Md Shamsed Chowdhury. Together with Judith's husband, Mohamed, the three of them delivered election leaflets and canvassed voters in all the possible Labour areas in Hyde Park Ward, particularly in the social housing blocks.

Brought up in rural Cumbria and educated at a Quaker school, Judith trained as a nursery nurse in Edinburgh before moving to West Yorkshire where she changed career direction and started to work first, as bus conductor, and then as a driver, including driving coaches for National Express. In the 1980s she returned to the care profession and trained as a nurse, moving to London to work at Paddington Green Children's Hospital. Later, Judith worked abroad in Iraq and Libya for a few years. Now retired, she spent over a decade working at a hospice in Clapham.

The initial 'campaign meeting' was very positive. Judith and I got on straight away. Both from the North, we spoke plainly about our very limited prospects and both knew that what we were about to embark on was a real 'long shot'. But we were both determined to give it our best. Patrick was delighted that he had two potential candidates willing to put in the work. We discussed who might be our third candidate and the name of Paul Fisher, a recent mover into Talbot Square from Camden, came up straight away. Paul was an experienced Labour member, a barrister and keen to get involved. We agreed I should sound him out and the next day he agreed to put himself forward with little need for persuasion.

A few days later, I wrote our first '10-point campaign plan' with my thoughts on priorities, which were very focused on "getting things done".

"1. Everyday issues of refuse collection, potholes, cracked pavements, defective streetlights and other matters should be central to the campaign, not least because we can actually get things done. We should take photos and encourage residents to send us photos of hotspots so we can show 'before' and 'after' photos on the website.
2. In some parts of the ward, development pressures will be a major concern of residents, whether it is redevelopment or extensions. Taking up residents' concerns will get us their support even if we cannot stop the developments getting permission. Monitoring building sites and taking up transgressions will also be important.
3. We should run three separate but linked campaigns to reflect the different issues and demographics - (1) the Hyde Park Estate area bounded by Edgware Road/Bayswater Road and Sussex Gardens (2) the Star Street area between Sussex Gardens and Praed Street and (3) the Paddington

Basin/Sheldon Square area - to keep things hyper local. Most people are only concerned about their local patch and we should show that we know every cracked pavement.

4. We should concentrate on the nuts and bolts of getting the vote out. So, we should use our current voter ID to write to every Labour supporter to encourage them to sign up for a Postal Vote (PV). We should also ask them for their email so we can send them our regular newsletter.

5. We should spend some time in the new part of the ward and with new voters - knocking on doors, delivering leaflets and looking for local environmental issues. We should start to get to know Labour supporters in the Chapel Street/Hyde Park Mansions triangle and the new residents in Dudley House and encourage them to get PVs.

6. We should aim to send out an email Action Report each month and use the content to prepare printed versions for the three local areas as often as practical.

7. We could undertake a survey amongst Mews dwellers asking for their priorities for action - better lighting, improved street sweeping/refuse/recycling, more policing of ASB, etc.

8. We should use Facebook to reach out to more people by regular posts which we spend money on boosting to the relevant postcodes. We know how much time we spend knocking on doors that are never answered and this might be a better way of making contact.

9. We could use Instagram in a similar way and post short YouTube videos highlighting the issues we are taking up

10. Finally, we need to tell our individual stories about ourselves so we define who we are, rather than the Tories defining us

The next day, Margaret Lynch set up a Facebook page for the Hyde Park Labour Action Team and a Gmail account. 'Operation Hyde Park' was gearing up for action. The 10-point plan formed the basis of the next 12 months' campaigning.

****

Meanwhile, on 14th March, following the Queen's Park Ward candidate selections, I made public my decision to step down from the Council in May 2022. I tweeted;

"By May 2022 I will have served for 33 years as a Westminster City Councillor, including 14 years as Leader of the Opposition. Time to hand the torch to a new generation. A privilege to be a Labour Councillor for Queen's Park who I will continue to represent for the next 12 months"

I received some very kind responses. Karen Buck MP called me *"one of the heroes of local government"*, Westbourne Labour Candidate Angela Piddock said, *"you made a difference"* and Maida Vale Councillor Nafsika Butler-Thalassis said, it *"shows how much can be achieved even in opposition"*. Prophetically, Labour Group Leader Adam Hug commented, *"I hope the Tories don't think he is going to go easy on them over the final year"*.

I also received an unexpected email from the Leader of the Council, Councillor Rachael Robathan who wrote, *"We may not agree on many things, but I know that we both love this great City of ours and I know you have always fought for your residents and ward. We don't have to share the same views to be able to respect others who've worked incredibly hard for many years for Westminster. I know you'll be missed."*

The next day, on 15th March, I put out a fuller statement, *'Time to hand the torch to a new generation'*. I said,

"By May 2022 I will have served for 33 years as a Westminster City Councillor, including 14 years as Leader of the Opposition. It is time to hand the torch to a new generation. It is a privilege to be a Labour Councillor for Queen's Park who I will continue to represent for the next 12 months.

In May 2022, I will have been a Queen's Park Councillor for 25 years, with 8 years before that representing Harrow Road from 1982-1990. I am delighted that Cara Sanquest has been

selected to take my place to join Patricia and Hamza as Labour Councillors.

I have enjoyed being a Queen's Park Councillor since I was elected in 1997, representing a diverse community, getting things done and standing up for people when they are getting a raw deal from Westminster Council and other organisations. I have made a lot of friends and I hope to stay in touch with as many as possible.

During my years as Leader of the Labour Group, from 1987-1990 and 2004-2015, I experienced politics at the sharp end. Leading the team that exposed the 'Homes for Votes' scandal in the 1980s and helping to recover some of the lost money from Shirley Porter in the early 2000s, stand out as the most high-profile. I look back on my time as Chair of the Education Scrutiny Committee in 2001-2003 as the most successful. The Committee undertook a review of secondary education, leading to the creation of Westminster and Paddington Academies, both which are excellent schools, giving a great start in life to young people.

I am not going away and hope to pass on my experience to others. And for the next year or so I will remain in top gear."

So, what would the next 12 months bring?

Chapter Two – Try Again. Fail again. Fail better

Westminster City Council has been ruled by the Conservative Party since its formation in 1964 through a merger of the former Westminster City Council and the Metropolitan Boroughs of Marylebone and Paddington. Apart from a brief two-year period between 1945 and 1947 when Labour ran Paddington Borough Council, all three Councils had been Conservative ruled since the creation of the Metropolitan Boroughs in November 1900.

Westminster Labour Party has had hopes of winning the City Council since 1986 when the Party won 27 of the Council's 60 seats and failed to become the largest party by just 106 votes. That herculean political effort sparked the Conservatives' notorious 'Homes for Votes' scandal when Council Leader Lady Shirley Porter and her Conservative colleagues tried to gerrymander future Council elections by moving likely Labour voters out of marginal Wards and selling their Council homes to people who were more likely to vote Conservative. This illegal political manoeuvre, combined with the lowest Council Tax in the country, had served the Conservatives well.

Since the Labour 'high water mark' of 1986, the Conservatives had enjoyed huge majorities over Labour at every election, no matter which party was in power nationally. A glance at the Council election results since 1990 gives a very clear picture, with Labour improving its performance in both 2014 and 2018, but still a long way behind the Conservatives:

1990 - Labour: 15 seats Conservative: 45 seats
1994 - Labour: 15 seats Conservative: 45 seats
1998 - Labour: 13 seats Conservative: 47 seats
2002 - Labour: 12 seats Conservative: 48 seats
2006 - Labour: 12 seats Conservative: 48 seats
2010 - Labour: 12 seats Conservative: 48 seats

2014 - Labour: 16 seats Conservative: 44 seats
2018 - Labour: 19 seats Conservative: 41 seats

In the run-up to the 2018 Council elections, Labour put huge efforts in to winning additional Council seats and it was clear that we were putting the Conservatives under pressure. Independent Soho resident, Andrew Murray, wrote in his 'State of Soho' blog in December 2017, *"Westminster Council election results have usually been a foregone conclusion. But there are signs that the 2018 local elections could be different."* Andrew noted *"that, despite always belonging to the ruling party on the council, and often being the party of national government too, Soho has struggled to see any great benefit from our Conservative councillors. We've been ignored, overlooked and neglected by the council – or else, as now, massively exploited."*

Andrew Murray continued, *"In Soho (and, my impression is, across the borough as a whole) there has been a significant and consistent upsurge in activity by the Labour Party. For years it seemed, at least from the vantage point of Soho, as if Cllr Paul Dimoldenberg was carrying the opposition banner more or less single-handed, raising issues (albeit from a distance) that concerned Soho residents. At election times, there was very little local Labour presence (or Conservative, for that matter). During 2017, however, it became clear that Labour were taking the West End ward seriously, as their Labour Action Team increasingly made its presence felt."*

Andrew Murray concluded his election analysis:

"Soho needs councillors who will be active on the ground, identifying problems and solutions, then energetically committing themselves to speaking up for and then achieving positive change for the people who live here. For a long time, Westminster Conservatives as a whole have paid more attention to the interests of business than to residents. If Labour can capitalise on this, in Soho and elsewhere, then the 2018 elections could be much more interesting than usual."

As a long-standing writer on London politics, Dave Hill's view on Labour's prospects was equally positive, but sensibly caveated by the scale of the task. *"Looking at the results from three-and-a-half years ago, Labour would need to overhaul margins of around 400 votes or more in a string of wards to pull off a sensational result,"* he wrote in his 'On London' blog in December 2017. *"But on an optimistic view around a dozen seats could well be in play, and that's enough to make Conservatives nervous."*

The hard work paid off and the 2018 Council elections delivered gains for Labour, the most spectacular being in the West End Ward where, after a two-year campaign, Pancho Lewis was elected as the first-ever Labour Councillor for the Ward and his running mates, Patrick Lilley and Caroline Saville were only narrowly defeated. In the Bayswater Ward, Maggie Carman won a seat for Labour for the first time since 1986 and in Maida Vale Ward, Labour's Geoff Barraclough and Nafsika Butler-Thalassis won the two remaining Conservative seats to join Rita Begum and take all three seats.

Still a long way behind, we looked forward to the Local Government Boundary Commission for England's review of ward boundaries, a process which happens every 20 years to take account of population movements within boroughs. There had indeed been significant population movements in Westminster since the early 2000s, not least in the increase in residential development. The significant issue in Westminster is that only a limited number of the new flats that have been built are occupied by long-term residents. Many are the homes of foreign nationals who are not qualified to vote. Some are second homes of UK and foreign nationals and only occupied for a few months a year. Others are investments and not occupied at all. The huge disparities in population are clearly evident in the Electoral Register where, for example, the Knightsbridge & Belgravia Ward had just over 4,000 electors in 2020, compared with over 7,000 in the north Paddington Wards of Queen's Park and Harrow Road.

In looking forward to the next Ward boundary review, which is based significantly on the estimated future population arising from new developments, we were at pains to point out the particular local circumstances at play, with no guarantees that new developments would be occupied by people eligible to vote or occupied at all. Despite making detailed representations to the Local Government Boundary Commission for England on this point, the LGBCE chose to ignore the clear evidence, claiming;

"The Labour Group expressed concern during consultation on our draft recommendations on how the Council had developed its electoral forecasts and we noted these concerns. However, as stated in our guidance, electoral forecasting is not an exact science, and we have carefully considered the information provided by the Council and the Labour Group. We are satisfied that the projected figures remain the best available at the present time. We have used these figures to produce our final recommendations."

The final recommendations of the 2019 review of Wards by the Local Government Boundary Commission for England were very disappointing for Westminster Labour Party. Both political parties had agreed that the number of Councillors should be reduced from 60 to 54 and we had put forward a range of three and two member Wards that we believed better reflected local communities than the current arrangements. We also thought that our proposed new wards would maximise our chances of electing additional Labour Councillors. However, the LGBCE agreed with the Conservative proposals (disguised as the Council's proposals) to retain three member Wards and the current pattern of Wards across Westminster.

When the draft LGBCE recommendations were published in late 2019, we were devastated; the prospect of continued one-party rule in Westminster was staring us in the face for the next four years at least. But being very much a 'glass half full' political party, our thoughts turned to other strategies and the idea of campaigning for a directly elected Mayor for Westminster, which we had considered in the past, was revived. In January 2020, I wrote a paper, *'Time for change in Westminster – why we need an elected Mayor'*, which I presented to Westminster North Labour Party General Committee. I argued,

"The draft LGBCE ward boundary proposals look likely to continue to entrench the Conservatives' control of the Council to the extent that Labour could win a majority of the popular vote in 2022 and yet the Conservatives could again win a majority of Council seats. This is exactly what happened in Wandsworth in 2018, when Labour won 42,401 votes compared to the Conservatives' 42,002. Yet the Conservatives continue to run the Council with 33 seats to Labour's 26."

I concluded, *"A Labour-run Westminster Council in 2022 based on the new ward boundaries would be a terrific result, but if the electoral system makes that difficult, an elected Labour Mayor would be just as effective."* The General Committee agreed with this 'Plan B', but before we could arrange to collect the signatures to force a referendum on the proposal, Covid 19 intervened and put a stop to all campaigning.

Announced in May 2020, the LGBCE final decision to reduce the number of Councillors from 60 to 54 had one significant benefit for Labour. The loss of 6 Councillors would hit the Conservatives hard, particularly in Marylebone and Pimlico. In Marylebone, two strong Conservative Wards (Marylebone High Street Ward and Bryanston & Dorset Square Ward) were reduced to just one very strong new Conservative Marylebone Ward. And in Pimlico, two Conservative Wards (Warwick Ward and Tachbrook Ward) were replaced by a new Conservative Pimlico North Ward. This was great cause for celebration, as was the addition of the northern part of Fitzrovia to the West End Ward.

However, on the negative side for Labour, the new Pimlico South Ward, along the Thames riverside and centred on the Churchill Gardens estate, would lose the Labour-voting Peabody and Ebury Bridge estates and gain the 1,100 apartment Dolphin Square block, traditionally a Conservative stronghold. This, in our view, would make Pimlico South a tough Ward to hold on to. To make matters worse, the new boundary proposals for Bayswater and Lancaster Gate Wards made both Wards more likely to elect Conservative Councillors. The new Bayswater Ward had a large part of Conservative-voting Lancaster Gate transferred into the south of the Ward. While the Lancaster Gate Ward received an additional set of Conservative voters in the Westbourne Terrace area, together with the small Brewers Court Council estate close to the Westway.

David Boothroyd got straight to work on the new Ward boundaries and produced a 'best estimate' of election results had the 2018 election happened on 2022 boundaries. David argued, *"The change in West End is enough for us to have won two seats instead of one, but we would not have taken any Bayswater or Pimlico South seats"*. On a more positive note, he observed that although the new Wards *"does mean the council proportions would have been the same on 2018 results, they have left a more even distribution of votes which means a 5% swing is enough for Labour to win the council (down from 6.5% on previous boundaries)."*

David's initial reaction to the new Ward boundaries was, *"May be a bit early to talk about targets but Pimlico South is not out of reach. Might also be worth a practice run during the GLA election next year targeting uncanvassed bits of the new Hyde Park."*

Looking more closely at David's estimates for the share of the vote for each of the new Wards, the figures did not look good and confirmed our worst fears.

The new Bayswater Ward estimates showed the Conservatives winning all three seats with 43.8% of the vote and Labour winning 34.1% and Lib Dems on 19.6%. The new Lancaster Gate Ward was similarly bleak with David's estimates giving the Conservatives all three seats with 47.9% of the vote, compared to Labour's 37.1% and 14.3% for the Lib Dems.

In Pimlico South, the story was similarly unhelpful with the David's estimates showing the Conservatives winning all three seats in Pimlico South with 48.3% of the vote compared to Labour's 42.9% and the Lib Dems at 8.3%.

The only bit of joy was in the new West End Ward where David's estimates showed us winning two of the three seats, with 42.5% of the vote compared to the Conservatives' 41.4% with 7.4% to the Lib Dems.

Overall, David's predictions showed the Conservatives winning 37 seats to Labour's 17 seats, giving the Conservatives a 20-seat majority. This was deeply disappointing and far from what we had hoped for. What made the situation even more galling was, in terms of the popular vote, the 2018 Council elections had seen the Conservatives hold on to power with a massive 22-seat majority, with just 42.8% of the vote compared to Labour's 41.1%. We faced two tough years of campaigning with little prospect of electing additional Labour Councillors, let alone winning control of the Council. Even for a 'glass half full' Westminster Labour Party, the prospects were dire.

****

So, how were we going to deal with this new challenge, if at all, to end the '58 years of pain'?

West End Councillor Pancho Lewis, who had sensationally won one of the three West End Wards in 2018, was not deterred by the new boundary changes. In November 2020, he wrote to Labour Councillors suggesting a very focused approach to the 2022 Council elections. *"To have a chance of winning, we must,"* he argued, *"be ruthlessly focused".* He suggested a four-point plan:

- *Ditch campaigning in seats where we can't realistically win.*
- *Get Labour voters on the postal vote, starting with Labour members in each target ward*
- *Build 6 Action Teams in six target ward seats (West End, Bayswater, Pimlico South, Little Venice, Vincent Square, and Lancaster Gate) whilst continuing to work in Maida Vale ward. Team members need to be highly motivated, competent, and committed.*
- *Have a very simple message that resonates with voters and persuades them to vote for us*

Pancho categorised the wards in winnability with the aim of winning at least 28 of the 54 seats on the Council

- Four Solid Labour Wards - Queens Park, Harrow Road, Westbourne and Church Street Wards (12 seats)
- One Likely Labour Ward– Maida Vale Ward (3 seats)
- Three Split Wards – West End, Bayswater and Pimlico South Wards (9 seats)
- Three Likely Tory Wards – Little Venice (Labour 200 votes behind), Vincent Square (Labour 300 votes behind) and Lancaster Gate (Labour 250 votes behind) Wards

Winning the four solid Labour Wards, one Likely Labour Ward and the three 'split' Wards would give us 24 seats. To win four more seats, we would have to take them from the Conservatives in the Little Venice Ward (which Labour last won in 1986) and Vincent Square and Lancaster Gate Wards, neither of which had ever been represented by Labour. This was a huge challenge at a time when the new ward boundaries gave us little assistance.

A key issue for us was the 'message'. For over 30 years, the Conservatives had their very own *'very simple message that resonates with voters and persuades them to vote for us'* which we needed to find for Labour. The lowest Council Tax in the Country was a very potent electoral message, not just for Conservative voters, but for many Labour voters, too. Election after election, the Conservatives printed the same leaflets showing the low Council Tax figure for Conservative Westminster contrasting with the much higher Council Tax figure in Labour Camden, Brent and Lambeth. The message was very simple – 'Vote Conservative in Westminster or Labour will get in and hike your Council Tax to what your neighbours pay across the road in Camden, Brent and Lambeth'.

If we were to have any chance of picking up additional seats, let alone winning the Council, we had to neutralise the Conservatives' 'lowest Council Tax in the country' message. How to do this was the big question and was something which the Labour Group wrestled with over the coming months.

For Pancho and others, the choice was simple. We should pledge to freeze the Council Tax, at least for an initial period, so that we could promise there would be *'No Council Tax increase if Labour win'*. Backing up this argument was the fact that a 1% Council Tax increase raises around just £600,000, a very small sum in relation to the Council's budget. A 2% Council Tax increase (the maximum allowed without calling a referendum) would raise just over £1 million and would not transform the Council's ability to tackle deep seated issues. In addition, the Council Tax is not the biggest source of revenue for the Council. Income from the Council's parking operations raises considerably more money than the Council Tax. Indeed, the journalist Simon Jenkins once remarked that

Westminster Council was a very profitable parking company with a side line in providing local government services.

Some other members of the Labour Group took a contrary view and argued that, for us to be taken seriously as a potential ruling group, we could not go into an election pledging to improve local services and, at the same time, promising to freeze the Council Tax. *'Where will the money come from?"* would be the obvious first question voters (and the press) would ask. A more responsible approach to Council Tax, they argued, would be to limit Council Tax rises to inflation.

Then there were others who took a more pragmatic view. *"We are not going to win, everybody knows that, so what is wrong with saying we will freeze the Council Tax if it neutralises the Tory message and helps us win a few more seats?"* This approach had its supporters amongst the many Labour Councillors and activists who had struggled over the years with the potent Conservative message. After debates and discussions, always friendly and comradely, it was agreed to put forward the Council Tax freeze proposal for the first two years of a future Labour Council (2022/23 and 2023/24). Importantly, we decided that we would make this pledge early and repeat it as often as possible to get maximum opportunity to neutralise the Conservative Council Tax message.

Our argument was best articulated in March 2021 at the Council's annual budget meeting when we argued that *"this is not the time for a Council Tax rise, the Government should pay for vital local services."* Labour's Shadow Cabinet Member for Finance, Councillor David Boothroyd told the Council meeting,

"Now is not the time for tax rises. If the Government can find £22 billion for a failed test and trace system, they can find the money to protect the local services rather than asking hard pressed residents to foot the bill. If the Conservative Government has billions to spend on concealed contracts for

their chums, why can't they raise the cash to help councils rather than raising council tax?"

David continued,

"For the last decade Labour have supported Westminster Conservative's proposed Council Tax levels, while identifying examples of local waste and suggesting efficiency savings to help protect local services to those most in need in the face of Conservative cuts. We will continue to suggest new ways to protect Council services but this year, Labour will vote against the Council Tax rise proposed by Westminster Conservatives because we believe the Council should be sending a message to the Johnson Government that they should be the ones to fund vital local services at this unprecedented time."

As in previous years, we accepted the proposed increase in the Adult Social Care precept to limit the Council's cuts in care for the elderly and vulnerable, services that proved so vital during the pandemic.

In November 2021, we argued that, as Westminster's residents face a challenging winter with rising prices and energy bills, they want to know that they aren't going to have any nasty surprises in the spring in when it comes to Council Tax. Westminster Labour Leader Councillor Adam Hug said:

"The burden of Council Tax falls disproportionately on those most in need, so it is essential that at this difficult time for residents that the Council does all it can to keep Council Tax low. That's why Labour will vote to stop any rise in Council Tax until 2024 at the earliest."

In January 2022 we added to our Council Tax freeze argument by calling on the Council to freeze council rents to tackle cost of the living crisis. We argued that many Westminster residents are struggling with rising bills. People on low or fixed incomes are being hit particularly hard.

Councillor Liza Begum, Labour's Shadow Cabinet Member for Housing, said:

"At a time when we find ourselves going through a cost of living crisis, raising Council rents would be devastating to some of the most vulnerable in our community. People are finding it difficult to make ends meet and keep up with bills; now is the time to support residents, not burden them with higher Council rent."

And at the Budget meeting on 1st March 2022, Councillor Adam Hug, repeated our Council Tax freeze pledge, telling the Council meeting:

"Since November 2021, Labour have been campaigning for council tax bills to be frozen for the next two years to help residents during the Conservative cost-of-living crisis. Belatedly, the Conservatives have responded to our pressure and agreed to a freeze this April. However, they have said nothing about the future. This is why Labour has put forward an amendment to this year's budget demanding the council make plans for a freeze for next year (2023/24), funded by cutting back on spending on highly paid consultants. Labour has also introduced an amendment that would freeze council rents this year rather than raise them at 1% above (CPI) inflation as the Conservatives currently plan."

To further demonstrate Labour's financial responsibility, Adam called *"for the Council to hold a 'zero-based budget' review that goes line by line through the council finances to root out any future wasteful spending on projects that don't deliver on residents' needs."* While David Boothroyd underlined our commitment to 'balancing the books'. *"Westminster residents deserve a break from Conservative short-term fixes that do nothing to make the council business-like and instead waste money,"* he said. *"Our prudent proposals are residents' priorities: checking every penny the council spends to make sure we get the most from it. A Labour council would be focussed and efficient."*

Speeches at Council meetings and press releases are all very well, but we needed to get the 'Council Tax freeze' message out widely and often. So, every piece of election material from November 2021 had the 'Council Tax freeze' pledge prominently displayed. Repeating the message for six solid months was the only way we would get our message across to the voters to neutralise the Conservative 'trump card'.

Chapter Three – Operation Hyde Park

For the 'Operation Hyde Park' decoy ploy to be taken seriously by the Conservatives and encourage them to move people and resources in defence of one of their safest Wards, our campaign had to be real, visible and relentless. Talk would not be sufficient. It had to be backed by action.

But before we get into the detail of 'Operation Hyde Park', let's look at who lived in Hyde Park Ward to assess what was in store for us and the scale of the task.

According to the *'Hyde Park Ward Profile'* produced by the City Council, there were about 14,500 residents living in the Ward, of whom 17% were children and 12% were pensioners. There were just over 6,000 people registered to vote, with voter turnout at past Council elections at around 30%. Based on the electoral figures, we could expect about 1,800 people to vote and we would need about 900 votes to secure a winning 50% share of the votes. To put this in perspective, at the 2018 Council elections, the Conservatives won 48.4% of the vote, to Labour's 29.6%, with the Liberal Democrats on 11.5% and the Greens on 10.5%. Turning that around would not be easy.

The largest household groupings, according to Acorn types, were *'Younger professionals in smaller flats'* (3,100 households) and *'Metropolitan professionals'* (2,100 households). Households comprising *'Metropolitan money'* and *'Multi-ethnic purpose-built estates'* were much smaller with 500 and 300 households respectively. There were two student halls of residence along Sussex Gardens, including Imperial College's Wilson House.

With the growth of private renting in Westminster, we had noticed a real demographic change within the Labour Party locally, with more young professionals choosing to rent close to where they work and socialise. A decade or more ago, those same young professionals would have been thinking of buying their first home in outer London areas. The presence of so many young professionals was a positive change for our campaign.

A typically cosmopolitan inner London area, 32% of non-English speaking households spoke other European languages, with Italian and French the most common, followed by Arabic (26%), South Asian (19%) and East Asian (14%). With the ramifications of Brexit still having an impact, the presence of so many European nationals on the Electoral Register was also a positive sign. At the EU referendum in 2016, almost 69% of Westminster residents voted 'Remain'. We believed that many EU nationals would be instinctively negative towards the Conservatives.

The Index of Multiple Deprivation, based on official data, identified the northern parts of the Ward around Star Street and Paddington Basin as the most 'deprived'. We knew that this small 'core' of residents would vote Labour – if we could contact them and encourage them to vote. On their own, they were not nearly numerous enough to win, but without them we certainly could not win.

The Council's annual *'City Survey'* asked about resident satisfaction with the Council's services, with 56% *'very satisfied with the way Westminster City Council is running the City'*, compared to less than 40% citywide, and 32% *'fairly satisfied'*. Questions about satisfaction with *'pavement maintenance'*, *'refuse collection'*, *'street lighting'* and *'street sweeping'* all received 98% satisfaction scores.

If winning elections was all about *'emptying the bins, keeping the streets clean and the streetlights working'* we were doomed before we started. But we knew from our own experience, that survey statistics don't tell the full story and that we could use residents' concerns for these services to further our campaign.

Finally, *'City Survey'* questions to identify 'problems' revealed *'people using or dealing drugs' (58%), 'people begging on the streets' (26%) and 'noisy neighbours or loud parties' (21%)* as the most common problems experienced by Hyde Park Ward residents.

When asked to identify 'the issues you are concerned about', Hyde Park Ward residents identified *'Climate change' (61%), 'increase in inequalities' (57%) and 'People homeless on the streets' (53%)* as their top concerns.

This information gave us insight and understanding into the issues we needed to focus on over the coming 14 months, combining local and national matters, which we would need to weave into our campaigning.

****

Hyde Park Ward includes the Royal Park, but the Park is home to just a handful of the 6,000 electors. Everyone else lives in the streets and high-rise flats to the north of the Park. This would be the battlefield where we would be deploying our 'troops' and positioning our 'tanks' over the coming year.

Closest to Hyde Park and based on a Georgian grid pattern, the Hyde Park Estate covers 90 acres and is bordered by Sussex Gardens, Edgware Road and Bayswater Road. First developed in the nineteenth century, it originally belonged to the Bishop of London before being transferred to the Ecclesiastical Commissioners (who later became the Church Commissioners) in 1836. Once considered *'the wrong side of the Park'*, by the post-war period it was described as a *"faded residential area"* following many years of neglect and war time bomb damage. Chesterton Humberts, the Church Commissioners' managing agents claimed in 1954 that *'a blight is cast over the estate'*.

Following post-war discussions with the London County Council, Paddington Borough Council and the Church Commissioners, it was clear that the bomb-damaged Hyde Park Estate was in need of a total overhaul. Property journalist Oliver Marriott explained the Church Commissioners' plans to keep the existing pattern of the Estate, replacing the three and four storey terraces and mews properties with high rise residential blocks and new low rise terraced houses in between.

"With leases falling in the Commissioners decided to bring in an architect, Anthony Minoprio, to draw up a general plan for the whole area and rebuild en bloc. They enlisted three partners – Wates, Max Rayne's London Merchant Securities and Great Portland Estates. Relatively little private residential development had been attempted inside London since the war for fear of politics and the high cost of building, so that the provision of £12 million worth of 763 flats and 112 houses involved a big risk."

Marriott also described how, *"in one corner the Commissioners launched out on their own and developed their first 100% controlled project at a cost of £4 million: the Water Gardens. Finished in the spring of 1966, 228 of the 238 flats in this pleasant development were let by the spring of the following year, a remarkably high rate of success."* Between 1955 and 1970, new high rise residential developments at Norfolk Crescent, 25 Porchester Place (at the time the tallest private residential tower in London), The Quadrangle, Devonport and Sussex Square changed the area beyond recognition.

Behind the Tyburn Convent on Bayswater Road lies St George's Fields which was a burial ground from 1763, and later used for archery, games and as allotments. The land was owned by St George's Church in Hanover Square, which sold it to developers in 1967. The 2.5-acre churchyard was developed in the early 1970s by The Utopian Housing

Association as a five-storey residential complex of 300 flats set in a private garden, complete with a few of the original tombstones.

Along the Edgware Road, the 1920s and 1930s saw a great deal of redevelopment with residential mansion blocks such as Park West, Cambridge Court and Portsea Hall replacing the traditional terraces and mews. In the 1990s onwards, the southern part of Edgware Road grew to be a centre for the Middle Eastern community, with many Lebanese restaurants opening and many Middle Eastern nationals buying flats in the mansion blocks along Edgware Road. As the BBC reported in December 2022, *"Famous for its Middle Eastern restaurants and Arab community, London's Edgware Road has been erupting into lively scenes as Morocco continues to make World Cup history. Morocco supporters took to the streets last week with flares and flags as the team knocked Spain out on penalties."*

The oldest part of the ward (and the most recently redeveloped) was the Paddington Basin area which was one of main gateways to Georgian London. The Paddington arm of the Grand Union Canal opened in July 1801 and joined with the Regent's Canal at Little Venice in 1820. The 'superhighways' of their time, the canals were the engine of economic growth bringing goods and coal from the industrial areas of the north and midlands. The area around Star Street developed as a response to this new prosperity and economic activity. The development of Paddington Station which moved to its current location in 1854, changed the area again, making it a busy and vibrant area, also bringing with it the usual undesirable features of life around a main line station.

The Star Street area was a well-known 'red light' district for much of the first half of the twentieth century and was one of the first areas to benefit from the start of the housing association movement in the 1960s. In 1965, Paddington Churches Housing Association (PCHA) was formed and set about renovating run down properties in Star Street and St

Michael's Street. Many families in the Paddington area were living in poor and extremely overcrowded conditions, often without even basic facilities. With two vicars among its seven founding members, PCHA's aim was "to provide homes at low rent for needy Paddington families" in the newly refurbished properties.

The 11-acre Paddington Basin site was redeveloped in the late 1990s and early 2000s, coinciding with the arrival of the Heathrow Express at Paddington Station.
The canal basin was drained, cleaned and repaired and the Merchant Square area developed with hundreds of new homes, headquarters offices for the likes of Marks & Spencer and others, together with bars, restaurants and cafes.

The Paddington Goods Yard site, which was demolished in 1986, was redeveloped at the same time as the adjacent Paddington Basin site. Called Paddington Central, the new development, designed by architects Siddell Gibson, included new flats at Sheldon Square, offices, shops and more cafes, bars, restaurants set around a landscaped amphitheatre and canal boats.

Set in the middle of the new developments rising from the canal side area are two of London's major pieces of social and economic infrastructure – St Mary's Hospital and Paddington Station.

St Mary's Hospital is the major acute hospital for north-west London, as well as a maternity centre and one of four major trauma centres in London, in addition to its 24/7 Accident & Emergency department. This is our local hospital where our daughters Amelia and Zoe were both born. Founded in 1845 on 'Christian and genteel values' it was the last of the great voluntary hospitals established in London.

The hospital building was erected 1843-61, and it was in a second-floor laboratory where Alexander Fleming discovered penicillin in 1928. Another well-known St Mary's alumni was neurologist Sir Roger Bannister, the first person to run a sub-four-minute mile, who did his training at the running track at nearby Paddington Rec. The private Lindo wing opened in November 1937 and has seen many royal births, including Prince William in 1982, Prince Harry in 1984 and more recently, Princes George and Louis and Princess Charlotte.

Relics of the area's past are still visible, with the multi storey stables for the many horses that worked on the railways at Paddington in use today as a research laboratory.

Paddington Station was the London terminus of the Great Western Railway and designed by Isambard Kingdom Brunel. Opened on its present site in 1850, Brunel's use of wrought iron and glass in the three-span roof was heavily influenced by the design and construction of the Crystal Palace for the Great Exhibition of 1851 where Brunel had been a member of the design committee. At the time, it was the largest train shed roof in the world. The Great Western Hotel was built along Praed Street and dates from 1854. It was the grandest hotel of its day, as well as the largest, with more than 100 bedrooms.

As everyone knows, Paddington is also the name of Michael Bond's famous bear. It is said he saw a small bear sat alone in the window of a shop at Paddington Station which he bought as a present for his family. Ten days later, Bond wrote his first Paddington book, which was published in 1958.

Other famous residents of Hyde Park Ward include political figures Winston Churchill at Sussex Square, his father Lord Randolph Churchill at Connaught Place, Lady Violet Bonham-Carter in Hyde Park Square and W.H. Smith, newsagent and Member of Parliament, in Clarendon Place. More recently, Tony and Cherie Blair bought a house in Connaught Square after leaving Downing Street.

From the arts, William Makepeace Thackeray lived in Albion Street, opera singer Richard Tauber lived in Park West and ballerina Marie Taglioni lived in Connaught Square. Sir Giles

Gilbert Scott, architect of Battersea Power Station, Waterloo Bridge and the red phone box, lived in a house he designed himself at the corner of Clarendon Close, a few doors down from where TV cook Nigella Lawson lives. Other Hyde Park Ward residents from the large and small screens include Michael Caine, who lived in Albion Close in the 1960s and Claudia Winkleman, a current Connaught Square resident.

And, of course, there was one further famous former Hyde Park Ward resident who was a Councillor for the Ward from 1974-1992 and Leader of Westminster City Council from 1983-91 – Dame Shirley Porter, who lived in a penthouse flat in Chelwood House on Gloucester Square. As I explained in *'The Westminster Whistleblowers'*, *"Her flat in Chelwood House was her 'breakfast office' to which harassed Council officers were summoned. The flat, likened to the lighting department at Selfridges, was described as 'indescribably vulgar' by former Conservative Councillor Patricia Kirwan. 'She had covers on the loo paper.'"*

Former Council Chief Executive Rodney Brooke told of one summons to Chelwood House where he noticed the bookcase boasted a complete set of the works of Sir Walter Scott. *"I see you share my taste for Walter Scott,"* I said to her. *'Walter Scott?"* she said. Clearly the name conveyed nothing to her. Disposing of the matter, she later asked me if I would like a gin and tonic. At the touch of a button, the spines of the complete works of Scott slid aside to reveal the cocktail cabinet."*

****

We started 'Operation Hyde Park' by getting to work on points 1 and 2 of the 10-point plan. First, we started by taking up everyday issues - refuse collection, potholes, cracked pavements, defective streetlights and other issues; and second, we took up residents' concerns about large development and construction projects. Judith, Shamsed and I met regularly at local cafes, usually at 'Panache' on Norfolk

Place, 'Arman's Kitchen' in Bathurst Street and 'Abasto' on Connaught Street, where we would be joined by local Labour members Jennifer Sheridan, Paul Fisher, Paul Spence and Ananthi Paskaralingam to chat, share gossip and plan our campaign.

Our first *'Hyde Park Matters'* newsletter was a 'Mews Special', which we delivered to about 400 mews properties, and included a survey asking for views on local issues. Walking through the many Mews in the ward was very enjoyable and a very good way of getting to know the 'nooks and crannies'. Importantly, unlike the mansion block apartments with concierges and security guards, every mews house had a front door letter box through which we could deliver our newsletters.

Our first 'big issue' came very soon. Unite Students were consulting residents on proposals to build a massive 840-bed student hostel on the Travis Perkins site, at the entrance to Paddington Basin, across the canal from 200 flats at Sheldon Square. Residents had already attended the initial consultation arranged by Unite and expressed their very strong opposition.

At the end of March 2021, I attended a Q&A webinar with the Unite development team to ask questions and make comments. I asked if there would still be the same demand for new student accommodation in the post-Covid world, particularly from overseas students. I followed that up by commenting that the proposed building took up most of the site and looked out of scale and unsuited to this very restricted site. I asked what the effect would be of building another tall building directly opposite Sheldon Square. I also asked how Sheldon Square residents' light would be affected and whether the development would create a narrow and windy 'canyon' along the canal, making it uncomfortable for pedestrians.

We posted these questions and comments on our *'Hyde Park Ward Labour Action Team'* Facebook page which provoked a very quick reaction from a couple of residents who thanked us for our support and interest in their battle. We also produced a *'Hyde Park Matters'* newsletter which Margaret Lynch designed and arranged the printing. I arranged to meet one of the residents to see how we could help them further and soon after we submitted a detailed written objection to the Council to the Unite/Travis Perkins proposals. In our letter to the Council, we set our five objections to the proposals,

Our first objection was 'Gross overdevelopment of the site'. We argued that *"the defining feature of the Paddington Basin area is the Canal and the development of new buildings along the Canal should respect this clear and defining context."* IWe also argued that *"the proposed 'stepped' 7–22 storey proposal is a contrived design which inherently admits that it is inappropriate for such an important and sensitive site. It is the wrong building in the wrong place."*

Our second objection was that the proposal was 'Out of scale with the low-rise residential Little Venice section of the Canal'. We made the point that, *"the proposed 22 storey building would ruin the current pleasant Little Venice section of the Canal environment which is characterised by a collection of modern low and mid-rise developments."*

Third, we argued that the proposals would 'Create an overbearing 'canyon' effect', which would *"create an overbearing and depressing 'Canyon' along this part of the Canal. The canal side walkways, cafes and bars would become less enjoyable to visit. The moored barges would be dwarfed and totally overwhelmed by the towering 22 storey building."*

Fourth, we said the proposal was 'The wrong use for the site'. While we supported the retention of Travis Perkins on the ground floor of the proposed development, we argued *"no justification is made for the proposed major student* accommodation development, beyond the general need for London." We also made the point that *"the overwhelming residential need in Westminster is for more homes for those who need to rent or buy a home locally. The site could provide the opportunity for more homes and it is of real surprise that this opportunity is not being taken."*

Finally, we agreed with residents that the site was 'Not an appropriate location for 840 students', making the point that *"Sheldon Square residents have, for many years, lived above the many bars and restaurants that create regular late-night noise and disturbance. How can it be reasonable or fair to add a further 843 potential customers to the local bars and restaurants, when it is abundantly clear that the available public and private provision cannot cope?"*

We posted our objection on the Westminster Labour website and sent links to Sheldon Square residents so they could see that we were on their side and actively campaigning alongside them. We also wrote to the *'Westminster Extra'*, the local weekly freesheet which printed our objection letter in full. Sheldon Square residents wanted to know what more they could do to make their objections heard and so we arranged a 'demonstration' outside their flats and encouraged residents to bring along home-made placards and banners.

On a hot and sunny afternoon in July 2021, Judith, Shamsed and I met about 30 residents and urged them to write letters of objection to the Planning Department and to contact the Mayor to ask him to refuse the application. Helpfully, the meeting with residents came on the same day as the Government announced a £64 million cut in funding to London universities which led credence to our view that the need for the 840 new student rooms was in doubt.

The scale of objections to the Unite/Travis Perkins was growing daily and our campaign on the side of residents was noticed by the Conservative Councillors in Hyde Park and Little Venice Wards who followed up with their own objection

letters, which were remarkably similar to ours. Unsurprisingly, in December 2021,
Unite/Travis Perkins decided to respond to the mounting objections by revising their proposals.

Unfortunately for them, it was too little, too late. We submitted a further objection to the revised proposals and told the local press, *"We are continuing to support local residents in their campaign against the revised proposals from Unite Students and Travis Perkins which in our view are very minimal: The proposed building is now stepped from 6 to 20 storeys, as opposed to the original proposal, which was 7 to 22 storeys. The number of student beds has been reduced from 843 to 768 – just 75 fewer."*

It was no surprise that the Unite/Travis Perkins revised proposals were unanimously rejected by the Planning Committee on 9th March 2022, just two months before the May Council elections. Speaking for Labour at the Planning Committee, Councillor Geoff Barraclough, shadow cabinet member for planning said, *"Everyone accepts that this site needs redevelopment but, given the residential flats already built close by, this proposal is much too tall. Travis Perkins needs to go away and have a complete rethink."* I was delighted to tell the local press, *"This is a victory for Sheldon Square residents with whom we have been campaigning against these proposals for over a year. A development of 20 storeys so close to the Sheldon Square flats would have done huge damage to residential amenity."*

Over the year we had delivered five *'Hyde Park Matters'* Labour newsletters to Sheldon Square residents and had built up our credibility, demonstrated our leadership and helped to secure a famous planning victory. Over time, we also picked up other issues on which we helped residents, particularly amongst the housing association tenants who lived in the first two floors of Sheldon Square. We also got to know some of the owners of the expensive flats on the upper floors, few of whom we expected to vote for us but who we reckoned might think about it if we showed we could 'get results' on local issues.

Collecting emails was also important as it enabled us to keep in touch with Sheldon Square and all other residents through our monthly *'Hyde Park Ward Labour Action Report'* email. We started with around 100 email addresses across the Ward when we started in March 2021, and this grew to nearly 600 by the time of the Council elections in May 2022. In addition, we posted our monthly *'Action Report'* on our Facebook page and paid to 'boost' the post to relevant W2 postcodes, thereby ensuring a much wider coverage.

It is difficult to over-estimate the influence of the regular *'Action Reports'* in building our profile, demonstrating our relevance and winning support. It was probably our biggest single campaigning asset. Every month we received a very positive reaction from residents. Typical comments were, *"Thank you for your wonderful emails which I enjoy reading every month"*, *"We've noticed in your recent updates your continued efforts to make our little street cleaner and better. Thank you"*, *"Thanks for your speedy action!"* and *"Thanks again for all you're doing, it is appreciated."* These were genuine comments and we knew we were making our mark.

****

While the Unite/Travis Perkins campaign was high profile, most of our campaigning was a great deal more 'everyday'. For example, in April 2021 we asked Notting Hill Genesis *"when the outside of 38-40 St Michael's Street will be repainted following the damage to the plaster and repair work on the façade of these houses. The current situation is clearly very unsatisfactory and needs urgent attention."*

In May 2021, we called for action on empty shops on Edgware Road urging the Council and Marble Arch Business Improvement District (BID) to work with property owners and landlords to bring the empty premises back in to use. In our letter, we said, *"These empty units need to be brought back into use, perhaps as 'pop-ups' to encourage new independent retailers and restaurateurs. Alternatively, these vacant premises could be occupied by artists or makers to showcase their works and provide an attractive and lively ground floor. Edgware Road is both a local high street and an international destination. Action needs to be taken to get these empty premises back into use to serve residents and visitors."*

In June, we reported on a success in Westbourne Street where we asked the Council if *"the area around the lamp post outside 20 Westbourne Street could be given a 'deep clean' as the pavement has a lot of ingrained dirt from the spillage from dumped rubbish bags."* A few days later, we were able to tell residents that the area around the lamp post had been given a thorough washing down and was now cleaned up. One of our techniques was to deliver letters to residents in the vicinity of the problem. First, we would tell them that we had reported the problem. If successful, we would send a follow up letter telling residents that the job had been done and inviting them to let us know if there were any other issues we could investigate.

We continued every week with the 'bread and butter' issues. In early July, we called on the Council to remove abandoned bikes in Portsea Place attached to bike stands. Later that month we supported residents who had been campaigning for almost a decade to have National Express coaches diverted from residential Westbourne Terrace to the shorter and non-residential Eastbourne Terrace, to bring residents some relief from the constant traffic noise and improve air quality on this busy road.

We organised a petition which argued, *"Now that Eastbourne Terrace is open following completion of the Crossrail works, we call upon Westminster Council and Transport for London to immediately arrange for National Express buses to use Eastbourne Terrace to benefit local residents."* The Westbourne Terrace area was transferring from Hyde Park

Ward into our target Ward of Lancaster Gate, so we were very keen to give practical assistance to our Action Team colleagues next door.

In August 2021, we were contacted by residents in Star Street who said, *"We've had to put up with five years of that horrid scaffolding on Cambridge Court! Do you know anything about it and could you pressure the owners of the building to remove it faster!"* We wrote to the developers of the site to urge a speedy end to the work. They told us, *"We apologise for the years the scaffold has been in place. The delay started about 5 years ago when we detected a major fault in the building. We then had the problem of the main contractor going into liquidation. We are now pleased to inform you the development is almost complete and the Star Street scaffold will be removed in the next few weeks."* We told residents that we would be watching closely to ensure that the developers keep to their word. To communicate progress on local issues like this, we got into the habit of posting a daily Facebook update on individual items that we were taking up on behalf of residents. We kept that up right up to Election Day.

Later in August 2021, we supported residents opposed to another major development in the Ward. This time it was a proposal to demolish The Chapel pub and the construction of a 7-storey hotel, directly adjacent to Wallace Court on Old Marylebone Road and Chapel Street. Again, we contacted residents by letter and told them that we had submitted an objection to the planning application following the publication of the Planning Officer's report recommending approval for the plans. In our letter we wrote, *"As your report correctly points out, "the development will have negative impacts particularly on the amenity of the adjacent residents in Wallace Court". Your report points out that, "a considerable number of these flats are single aspect and look out over the development site and will therefore be directly affected."*

We also supported residents' doubts as to the need for another hotel and said, *"we can understand residents' questioning the need for another hotel on Old Marylebone Road when there are two large hotels currently under construction just a matter of a few yards away. Surely the greater need is for more affordable homes?"* We also expressed our disappointment *"that the opportunity to preserve what you describe as "the last remnant of early 1800's development in the area" was not considered by the architects. The opportunity should have been taken to preserve some of the existing public house within the new development, not least to make it stand out from the bland corporate architecture that often characterises modern developments."*

We were delighted when the Planning Committee decided to defer a decision and asked the Planning Officers to go back to the developers to negotiate changes that would deal with residents' objections. The next day, we wrote to residents giving them the good news that the Committee had listened to their concerns and all hope of defeating the plans was not lost. Not surprisingly, our efforts won us friends in Wallace Court, the residents most badly affected.

By September, we were making real strides forward, particularly on issues we had been taking up since the start of 'Operation Hyde Park'. At the request of residents, we continued to urge the Council to relocate the two benches at the corner of Southwick Street and Star Street. Residents said the benches attracted regular anti-social activity at night/early morning as well as litter and rubbish dumping. Much of the anti-social behaviour (ASB) around the benches occurred in the early hours of the morning, between 2am and 3am, when there are no police patrols. The ASB either involved drunk people resting around the benches and continuing their loud drunken conversations in the early morning or involving drug dealing and prostitution.

The area around Paddington Station had a long-established reputation for both prostitution and drug use and we made the point that *"it is surprising that both the Council and Police* appear to take a very relaxed view of the way that the location of these two benches simply encourages further ASB to the detriment of local residents." "Surely the relocation of these benches to somewhere more appropriate such as Norfolk Square," we argued "would be make good sense both in fighting ASB and improving the lives of residents."

In late September 2021, we asked the Refuse Team to clear the bins outside Alleyn Court on Sussex Gardens which had become overflowing with bags of rubbish and attracted dumping. We also asked if the collections could be increased to cope with the amount of waste and for fines to be issued to those responsible for the dumping.

Rubbish dumping was clearly a major concern for residents right across the Ward and this led us to develop a 5-point plan to tackle the issue here and in other parts of Westminster. We promised, "If Labour wins the city council elections next May, we will roll out a five-point action plan to get results for residents." The 5 points were:

- A "zero tolerance" policy of immediate fines for those responsible for rubbish dumping. The council's stated policy is to encourage "behaviour change" and that "the polluter pays". The current practice of sending "educational letters" to residents and business around dumping "hot-spots" is clearly having little impact. Heavy fines will certainly encourage "behaviour change" and ensure that "the polluter pays".
- CCTV cameras should be located at dumping "hot-spots" to catch those responsible. Other local councils do this and have succeeded in catching those responsible and publicising their details in the local media. Again, this will both change behaviour and make the polluters pay.
- Regular patrols of dumping 'hot spots' by city inspectors to signal to residents that this issue is a priority for the city council.

- *Closer liaison with landlords and estate agents to ensure that they know that they face heavy fines if they, or their tenants, or their building contractors, dump furniture, household goods, and builders' rubble on the pavement.*
- *Locating planters at known dumping 'hot-spots' to discourage dumping by "beautifying" the area. This worked very successfully at the Ashmore and Shirland Roads junction which used to be the worst dumping 'hot-spot' in Westminster and is now clear of rubbish as a result.*

Later that month, we continued with our 'pavement politics' by calling on the Council to 'deep clean' the Edgware Road, Porchester Place and Connaught Street pavements after repeated rubbish dumping at these locations. We also pointed out to the Council's Highways Team a poor section of the roadway on Somers Crescent where there was a very poor section of reinstatement which had left an uneven road surface. In October, we asked the Highways Team to fill three potholes on Southwick Street – one outside the 'Monkey Puzzle' pub and two others a few yards away outside The Quadrangle. We made the point in letters to residents in Southwick Street that, *"keeping local roads in good condition is an important part of caring for our local environment, as well as keeping them safe for pedestrians and cyclists."* A few days later we were able to tell residents, *"the potholes have now been fixed and filled in."* We were really demonstrating that 'we get things done'

In October, we also made friends with a new local group, Hyde Park Estate Residents (HyPER) which had been formed following a major 'falling-out' between members of the long-standing Hyde Park Estate Association (HPEA) after Small the Council's decision to scrap a proposal to introduce a Low Traffic Neighbourhood (LTN) in the area. The HPEA had objected to the LTN and those in favour of the proposal had left and formed their own local group, HyPER. This dispute had predated 'Operation Hyde Park' so we had no involvement for or against the LTN proposal.

We knew we had to be friends with both groups of residents so when HyPER started a series of events to support local businesses in October, we attended their first 'pop-up' party at the local cheesemonger, Buchanan's, in Porchester Place. We met some people we already knew, together with others who were delighted to meet us and expressed their support for an active Labour campaign in Hyde Park Ward. *"The Tories have had it too easy here for years and they take us for granted,"* was a familiar reaction *"it's great to see some opposition for a change."* And to make things even better, we sampled three excellent cheeses, including the legendary Mrs Kirkham's creamy Lancashire, together with a glass of fine cider. The cheese was so good I had to buy some to take home. Over the coming months we went to more of HyPER's 'pop-up' events with local businesses and widened our growing network of friends and contacts.

Our attention to local issues was relentless, but in a measured and manageable way. Our mantra was 'little and often'. We would take up local issues, most days of the week following short 'walkabouts' through the streets, squares and mews, taking photographs of things that needed fixing and talking to residents whenever possible. It took little time to report them to the Council, send a tweet and make a Facebook post. But it all added up and provided great content for our monthly *'Action Reports'*.

The more practical the issues needing fixing the better. In October 2021, we spotted a lamppost with the wires exposed on Chapel Street, near the side entrance to M&S, and asked the Street Lighting Team to arrange for it to be fixed. A by-product of 'Operation Hyde Park' was that things did actually get better. Following reports from residents about rubbish on the street in Harbet Road, we asked the Council to investigate the situation. There was indeed a problem. The Council told us, *"Harbet Road is privately owned and maintained so it isn't* included in the Council's street cleansing services. The council sweeps and cleans outside the red boundary line whilst the green area is cleaned and maintained by London Metropole. The Manager for the hotel stated that the area is cleaned between 11am and 7pm but could not produce a cleaning schedule to evidence this arrangement. The manager has agreed to instigate a more formal process to ensure cleaning of this area is carried out regularly. The area will be regularly inspected to ensure the Hotel is managing this area responsibly."

Another practical improvement came when we asked the Highways Team to remove or relocate the large signs on the pavement on Praed Street and London Street. Residents told us: "Two large notices have been on the pavement of the corner of the old London Street and Praed Street for more than a year. Given the flow of pedestrians in this area, they make walking on Praed Street quite perilous, let alone make any kind of social distancing possible. Removing those two large notices from the pavement would at least free up a bit of very needed space for pedestrians at the entrance of Paddington station." We got a very positive response from the Highways Team who said, "We have investigated the information signs on Praed Street near the junction with London Street in reference to Tanner Lane. We have today removed them as the new layout has been in place for over a year."

We told residents about this small success and they were full of praise, "I would not call it a small success, but a great success!' one resident said. "Thank you so much for your involvement, and congratulations on making this happen. I know it is not always easy to make the bureaucracy move. Thank you once again." We were getting more and more of this type of positive reaction from residents and it made us feel vindicated. Although we were not going to win, it was satisfying and motivating to know that our campaign was making a difference and that our efforts were noticed and appreciated by local people. We hoped they would tell their neighbours. We hoped, too, that some of them would even vote for us!

Another success came in December 2021 when the Southwick Street 'drug dealing' benches were relocated elsewhere. This had been a real triumph as, initially, the Council and Conservative Ward Councillors had resisted the move, saying that the local police had not requested the benches' relocation. However, we encouraged residents to write directly to their Conservative Councillors and to ask for the relocation of the benches. We reckoned that, with the Council elections just six months away, the Conservatives would be susceptible to resident pressure. And we were proved correct. In early December 2021, our campaign was successful, the Council removed the two benches at the corner of Southwick Street and Star Street which had for many years attracted regular anti-social activity at night/early morning.

I told the local press, *"This is a great success for residents and for the Hyde Park Labour Action Team. The relocation of these benches to somewhere more appropriate, such as Norfolk Square, makes very good sense, both in fighting ASB and improving the lives of Southwick Street residents."* We rushed out letters to residents to steal a march on the Conservatives who we expected would make the most of this. In the event, the Conservatives did nothing to capitalise on this popular decision. This particular failure encouraged us further. If they weren't bothered to 'bang their own drum', they were either running a very poor election campaign or, more likely, were very complacent that this sort of issue would have any impact on the result.

One of the benches was relocated by a bus stop on Norfolk Place, where it now provides welcome respite for people with heavy shopping or just a place to sit while waiting for a bus. This was probably one of the most valuable local improvements we helped to secure during 'Operation Hyde Park'. Small, but significant.

****

We started the New Year 2022 determined to increase our face-to-face contact with residents. In the previous few months, Judith and Shamsed had spent a great deal of time knocking on the doors of the 600 Park West apartments, encouraging eligible residents to register to vote and apply for a postal vote. Judith and Shamsed had made useful contacts in Park West during the 2019 General Election campaign and we thought that revisiting the block would help remind voters that we had a real concern for their problems.

Unauthorised short-term lets via Airbnb and other platforms was a very serious issue In Park West. In December 2018 the *'Financial Times'* reported that there were nearly as many bedrooms in Park West advertised on Airbnb than there were hotel rooms at The Ritz. According to the FT, the Council's Enforcement Team was investigating over 100 cases of suspected unauthorised short-term letting in Park West, bringing with it anti-social behaviour, noise, increased rubbish generation and worse. *"These people treat the place like a hotel because they have no interest, it's not their home,"* one resident told the FT. *"They are not being protective or careful about their baggage or whatever, the way they move in and out, the noise, the behaviour. They don't care what damage they do,"* he added. *"If they want to have a party, they'll have a party."*

For most of the time, our *'Action Team'* comprised the three of us together with Judith's husband, Mohamed and Dan, a young Labour Party Member who lived in Albion Street. Generally, we usually worked alone or in pairs, but from January 2002 we decided to go door-to-door as one group, partly to cover more ground, but also to present ourselves as a team, working together. We were joined by Judith's daughter and adult grandchildren, too, who came down at weekends from Yorkshire. It also helped that Shamsed spoke five languages (English, Arabic, Hindi, Urdu and Bengali) and could communicate easily with Middle Eastern and Asian residents in the Ward. We stressed again and again that everyone had three votes and you could apply for a postal vote if you weren't certain you would be at home or in the country on 5th May.

We also contacted friends and organised a few 'Action Days' when we boosted our number to eight or nine. I was very pleased when old friends Andrew Dismore, Linda Julian, Alan Lazarus, Jane Wilson and Paul Wheeler came out with us in Chapel Street and Sussex Gardens. We also encouraged contenders running to be the Cities of London & Westminster Parliamentary candidate to join us. Rachel Blake, the eventual successful candidate, was particularly keen to help, as were Deeba Syed and Awale Olad who helped us canvass residents in St George's Fields.

We also put a lot of effort into the Star Street area, where there were many properties managed by the giant and ever-expanding Notting Hill Genesis housing association. Since the 1960s when the housing association was first established, Paddington Churches Housing Association started to buy and improve houses in Star Street and St Michael's Street, creating homes for key workers at St Mary's Hospital in Praed Street. If there was a 'heartland' for Labour support in Hyde Park Ward, this was it and we wanted to maximise voter turnout in these streets.

Mixed in with the housing association homes were a number of owner-occupiers who had purchased and renovated rundown properties in the streets. Getting their support was important, too. Rubbish dumping was an issue in Star Street and, in January 2022, residents began putting up their own 'Don't Dump' signs which were promptly ripped down by Council Officers. Residents (and we) were shocked and angry that the Council had removed the 'Don't Dump' signs that residents had designed, paid for and attached to the lampposts at the corner of Star Street and Sale Place, next to the big black bins. The Council's excuse for removing residents' signs was *"the signs erected are not in keeping with our corporate standard, did not seek permission to use the council's logo".*

As one resident remarked, *"The signs did seem to make a difference, and it was easy to point to them and tell people it's illegal to dump. Last week I had to make a guy remove his broken-down wardrobe and he made the point that everyone else did it so he assumed it was okay. Since they have been taken down it's given people more agency to dump stuff there. The council's own signage has absolutely no utility in preventing dumping. These worked."* Another resident said, *"What a horrible red-tape world we live in. We are just trying to make a difference and help our community."*

I told the press, *"Residents are fed up with the lack of action from Boris Johnson's favourite Conservative Council and so they decided to take matters into their own hands by installing their own 'Don't Dump' signs at the Star Street dumping 'hotspot'. It really is a 'kick in the teeth' for local community action for the Council to rip the signs off the lampposts under the cover of darkness. The Council just ripped down the 'Don't Dump' signs and didn't even bother to put up their own Council signs."* There is no doubt that this thoughtless action by the Council lost support for the Conservatives and made it much easier for residents to think of us as a viable and credible alternative.

We also made strong efforts in the area around Paddington Basin which had undergone a massive transformation over the previous 20 years with major commercial and residential development. In addition to the social housing in Sheldon Square, new social housing had been built in Hermitage Street, Harbet Road and North Wharf Road as part of large private developments. Generally, around 25% of the new flats in the area were managed by housing associations. In addition, nearly 200 new 'intermediate' rent apartments at Dudley House had been built by the Council. Most of the new residents in Dudley House were young professionals and we hoped that our approach would appeal to their progressive and liberal outlook on life. We delivered newsletters and canvassed these residents regularly. We couldn't knock on doors in Dudley House, because of the tight security, so we stood outside speaking to residents as they came and went.

We also supported residents in the Paddington Basin blocks affected by the cladding scandal following the Grenfell tragedy. Residents in the Munkenbeck and Marshall private blocks on Hermitage Street and Montgomery House social housing on Harrow Road were covered in scaffolding for months while dangerous cladding was removed and replaced. Although we could only offer limited direct assistance, we supported residents' efforts to lobby Government and keep the issue in the public domain. We included news on the cladding issues in our regular *'Hyde Park Matters'* newsletters.

In February 2022 we continued our support for residents in Star Street who displayed pictures taken from CCTV of the illegal rubbish dumpers on a wall next to Number 1 Star Street as a way of deterring further illegal rubbish dumping. I told the local press, *"We applaud the efforts of Star Street residents in taking action to stop the illegal rubbish dumping in their street. We hope this initiative makes the illegal rubbish dumpers think twice before they dump their rubbish in the street. The Council needs to do more to support residents by getting tough with the rubbish dumpers, including the landlords and their agents who regularly dump furniture and household goods on the street."* We learned later that Star Street residents operated a WhatsApp group and the support we were giving residents were shared regularly, helping to build our support and credibility.

In the run up to the May elections we repeated our concerns about the decline of Edgware Road and called for a 'Plan of Action' to revive Edgware Road shops and restaurants. On our regular 'walkabouts' we counted at least 14 closed or empty shops and restaurants along Edgware Road. In addition, there were also empty retail and restaurant units in the new developments at Marble Arch Place and Regent House. We were very concerned that this number of empty retail and restaurant units was undermining the economic success and future of Edgware Road as a destination for visitors, as well as for long-term residents who valued the mix and diversity of the local shops and restaurants.

In our call for an action plan, we said; *"Edgware Road is an important retail and restaurant destination for residents and visitors. We are calling on the Council, local retailers and restaurants, landowners, including the Church Commissioners, Portman Estate, Marble Arch BID, residents' groups and local stakeholders to come together to discuss how Edgware Road's fortunes can be revived. We need a 'plan of action' to get Edgware Road back on its feet."*

****

Although Judith, Shamsed and I had been campaigning as the *'Hyde Park Labour Action Team'* since March 2021, by early 2022 we had not yet been adopted as Labour candidates for the May elections. This did not bother us unduly as the overriding point of our campaign was to draw the Conservatives to Hyde Park Ward and away from the West End. The main issue in the delay in arranging the selections were some familiar internal issues in the local constituency party. However, the selection was finally arranged for the evening of Thursday 3 February by Zoom. A shortlisting meeting attended by members of the Hyde Park Ward Labour branch was held on the evening of Thursday 27 January.

We were each invited to submit a statement, but we decided to submit a joint statement on behalf of the three of us, emphasising the fact that they were a team and wanted to continue as a team. We said:

"Labour needs to win Westminster Council so that we can:

- *build more Council homes for people in overcrowded conditions and for the homeless*
- *rebuild our youth services*
- *create more local jobs and training opportunities*
- *tackle crime and anti-social behaviour*
- *take strong action against illegal rubbish dumping on our streets*

Winning the Hyde Park Ward for Labour will be a tough call and that is why we have been campaigning hard over the past 10 months since March 2021, starting with the Sadiq Khan/Rita Begum Mayoral and GLA elections. We have delivered election material to every door in the ward. Since May we have continued our active local campaign by:

- *delivering five editions of our newsletter 'Hyde Park Matters' to every letterbox in the Ward - that's over 20,000 newsletters going to every corner of the Ward*
- *canvassing residents about their local concerns and taking up individual cases with the Council, housing associations and other organisations*
- *posting regular Facebook stories on the local issues we are taking up. These Facebook posts have reached thousands of residents, some of whom are hearing from the Labour Party locally for the first time*

We have shown residents that we are an effective, hard-working and determined Labour Team. All this direct and practical campaigning is getting results, with more and more residents saying they appreciate our efforts and will vote Labour in May. Residents compare Labour's no-nonsense approach with the lazy, complacent attitude of current and past Hyde Park Conservative Councillors."

We posted and emailed our statement to Labour Party members in Hyde Park Ward and, not leaving anything to chance, we started to contact them individually by phone and in person to encourage them to attend the selection meeting and vote for us. I was concerned about the shortlisting and selection meeting process after being alerted to an article written by the Chair of the Cities of London & Westminster Constituency Labour Party, Harry Stratton, arguing that people like me and my Labour Group colleague David Boothroyd *"have no place in local government"*. Harry was also a member of Hyde Park Branch Labour Party and would certainly be at the meeting arguing against my selection.

In his article in *'Jacobin'* in January 2022, Harry Stratton argued, *"In the UK, local governments are constantly agreeing to sleazy deals to provide hyper profitable contracts to property developers. The only solution: ban developers and their lobbyists from councils."* Picking out David and I for special attention, he continued, *"Westminster Labour's shadow chair of planning, David Boothroyd, moonlighted as the head of research for lobbyist Indigo Public Affairs, whose clients, he recognized, "are companies applying for planning permission from various local authorities" (although he claims he does not and would not work with clients in Westminster itself). Meanwhile, Labour's shadow cabinet member for city management, Paul Dimoldenberg, worked as chairman of a PR firm that "helps build a positive dialogue between local communities and our clients with planning, regeneration and development proposals." Or, put more prosaically, it helps developers lobby for planning permission."*

He concluded, *"The only solution is to ban property developers and their lobbyists from local councils, and from holding office in local political parties. This is an answer that center-left parties around the world have supported. But while Labour councillors are paid by lobbyists and property developers, nothing will change. Local government will remain a cesspit of sleaze, just on a slightly less grand scale."*

I was so angry by this personal attack. After all I had done to track down the illegal actions of Shirley Porter and her colleagues during the 'Homes for Votes' scandal, to be told that I had *"no place in local government"* was unbelievable. As expected, after I had made my 5-minute speech to the selection meeting, Harry Stratton launched his attack on me, with an accusation dressed up as a question. But to no avail. Hyde Park Labour members believed that I did have a place in local government. All three of us were selected and we were now officially Labour Candidates for Hyde Park Ward.

Chapter Four – An International Joke, London's Worst Attraction

All election campaigns need a high-profile issue which captures the essence of what the election is all about. Party strategists spend hours trying to find the elusive issue on which to base their election campaign. Often, they fail to find an issue or chose wrongly. But we were lucky. The Conservatives handed us the £6 Million Marble Arch Mound.

In February 2021, Westminster Conservatives unveiled plans to build a temporary 25-metre-high grass-covered mound at Marble Arch to attract shoppers back to Oxford Street following the pandemic. The Council claimed that the Mound would attract over 280,000 visitors in the six months it would open and that this would help to boost the Oxford Street economy. Crucially, the Council's financial estimates claimed that the £2 million cost to construct, manage and demolish the Mound would be covered by an £8 visitor entrance fee and an expected £450,000 in sponsorship. The Council report proposing the project also assured Councillors that sponsorship was *"considered conservative at this stage and could be substantially higher".*

The original idea for the Mound came from Elad Eisenstein, the Council's Director for the Oxford Street District project who told Councillors that a similar temporary project in Amsterdam had been very successful in attracting visitors. In his CV, Mr Eisenstein described himself as *"a member of the Mayor of London's Infrastructure Advisory Panel, he lectures widely on issues of cities, urbanism and sustainable design and publishes in leading UK and international magazines."* We later learned that the idea for a Mound was not new. In 2004, the Mound architects, MVRDV proposed covering the Serpentine Gallery in Hyde Park with scaffolding to create a mound. The project did not go ahead as it was decided that it would be too expensive and too difficult to deliver.

Surprisingly, the Council did not make this known to Labour Councillors at the time.

Not wanting to pour cold water on the Council's bizarre, but well-intentioned, proposal, we limited our initial criticisms to the practical arrangements and implications of building the Mound. We wrote to the Council asking for further information on the costs and details such as *"Will there be access for visitors with disabilities?"*, *"Where will construction traffic be routed?"* and *"What is the estimated number of lorries needed to carry the materials required to install and remove the mound?"*

West End Labour Councillor Pancho Lewis pointed out that, in addition to the logistical, operational and financial questions, we also needed to understand the environmental cost. *"This is a big undertaking and involves transporting masses of materials, only for it to be dismantled within half a year,"* Pancho commented. *"We need transparency and answers on these questions."* I backed up Pancho by telling the press, *"The future of Oxford Street is of critical importance to the Westminster economy and to tens of thousands of jobs of local residents. We need to think imaginatively and we also need to have proper regard to the practicalities and the impact on surrounding residential areas, as well as keeping a close eye on the costs involved. It is important that the Council is totally transparent about the costs and logistics involved in building and removing this temporary mound."*

The Council quickly approved the Mound and construction started in May 2021, but the danger signs started flashing when the Council failed to answer our relatively simple questions and soon the reality of the Council's promised *"verdant, tree covered"* mound with *"panoramic views across London"* became clear. As the July opening date got closer our concerns deepened. It was clear that the Mound would not be completed for 26th July official opening. There was no café or shop and the promised *"exhibition space for a new light-based art installation"* was nowhere to be seen.

More significantly, the look of the Mound was dramatically different to the artist's impression, with an obvious lack of the expected trees and plants. Even the basics, like tidying up loose cabling or enclosing the refuse bins had not been done. The public feedback was predictably dire. The *'Daily Mail'* branded it as a *"slag heap"* and a *"shit hill"*, while the *'Evening Standard'* called it *"London's Worst Attraction"* and the *'Metro'* labelled it a *"trash heap"*. The Conservative-supporting *'Daily Telegraph'* told its readers to *"Behold the £2m 'hill of rubble"* and in a stinging leader article described the Mound as *"A rather silly hillock"*, which must have left a bitter taste in the mouth for the Council's Conservative leadership.

It did not take long for the story to go international, with *'The New York Times'* writing that *"Londoners were promised a hill with a view, they got a pile of scaffolding"*. And then, the Mound went viral, becoming the target for thousands of online jokes and memes. Such was the negative reaction that the Council announced that, as it was not complete, admission to the Mound would be free in August. Predictably, the only reaction the Council could offer to this public relations disaster was to describe it as *"teething problems"*.

Equally predictable, we went into attack mode with Labour Leader Adam Hug saying, *"It is really worrying that Westminster Council doesn't seem to have got a grip of this flagship project that they had made the centrepiece of their efforts to revitalise the West End after the pandemic. The Council needs to urgently fix the outstanding defects with the Mound and undertake an urgent review about what went wrong. Taxpayers must not be left footing the bill for these failings if it misses its ticket targets."* Geoff Barraclough, Shadow Cabinet Member for Business and Planning, weighed in, too, *"The Mound has become a national, and now international, joke in less than 24 hours. This monument to municipal vanity has made a laughingstock of Westminster's leadership and brought the Council into disrepute.*

Westminster Council owes its residents an immediate apology for wasting £2m of their money on this folly."

The following day, 28th July, we launched a petition calling for an independent inquiry to answer a number of urgent questions. We asked, *"Why is the finished design lower than originally intended and at what point was it known that the view from the top of the Mound would not clear the tree line?".* We also called for an explanation for the delays, *"Who at the Council signed-off the project as ready to open when the café was not open, the exhibition not setup and the site was left scruffy with bins and cables everywhere?".* We also asked, *"When did the Council know the project was going to be unable to deliver the level of greenery promised in the promotional material?".* Crucially, we also called for an answer on costs, *"How much could local taxpayers lose if the Council fails to deliver its expected 280,000 paying visitors?"*

By now we were in top gear, fielding calls from the press, radio and TV and we were determined to make the most of this opportunity to broadcast the Conservatives' incompetence locally, national and internationally. We continued to feed the media interest by asking more questions to tease out the facts and figures of this fiasco. In early August we asked the Council a swathe of questions, including:

- *Can the council share revised projections for the number of paying attendees?*
- *What are the council's revised projections for total cost recovery? (particularly in light of the decision to make the mound free in August)*
- *If the council will not receive expected visitor numbers will the council be liable for covering the shortfall? (i.e. how much will taxpayers lose?)*
- *Are the council leadership aware of any concerns about the Mound raised by sponsors, stakeholders and officers prior to opening?*

- *Will Westminster Council agree to an independent investigation of its decision making and project management on the Marble Arch Mound project?*
- *Who are the project's sponsors? Is the proportion of the scheme expected to be covered by sponsorship the same as in the May Cabinet Decision? Are all sponsors under contract with the council? Are all sponsors obligated to provide the previously agreed levels of funding? Have any of the sponsors been invoiced? What discussions have taken place with sponsors since ticket sales were suspended? Does the council expect it will have to reimburse any sponsors?*

We were keen to put the Council's leadership failures under the spotlight and to demolish any pretence Westminster Conservatives had as competent and responsible stewards of public finances. Labour Group Leader Adam Hug said, *"There are some basic questions that the council needs to answer about what went wrong with its decision making and project management. These questions must be answered now but Labour believes there needs to be an independent investigation of what happened to ensure this fiasco isn't repeated."* Tellingly, there had been no statements or media appearances from the Council's Leader and its Deputy Leader about what had gone wrong. Never previously shy of the cameras, they disappeared from public view.

We didn't have to wait long to find out the reasons for the Council's silence. On 12th August the Council admitted that the true cost of the Marble Arch Mound had trebled to £6 million. The ruling Conservative Party's Deputy Leader Councillor Melvyn Caplan, who spearheaded the project, resigned his position. To add insult to injury, no decision was taken about a return to paid ticketing and we believed that the promised project sponsorship had failed to meet its targets, further raising the likelihood that Westminster residents will lose the full £6 million on the scheme.

We genuinely could not believe what was going on at City Hall. The Council was lurching from disaster to disaster. We demanded an urgent Scrutiny Committee meeting to investigate the situation. Labour Group Leader Adam Hug said, *"This latest stunning revelation clearly exposes the hubris, incompetence and unaccountability of Westminster's ruling Conservative administration who have allowed the Mound's costs to triple without telling anyone."* And with an eye to the Council Elections in May 2022, Adam underlined the wider implications for local residents with a message we repeated relentlessly for the next 10 months, week-in, week-out, *"The Conservatives have misled the public about the true cost of their folly and it is clear to everyone that it is time for a change in Westminster. Residents will have their opportunity at next May's Council Elections to hold Westminster Conservatives to account for their arrogance and mismanagement. The Tories just can't be trusted with taxpayers' money."*

The local fall-out in Westminster to the news that the cost of the Mound had trebled to £6 million was quick and brutal. A week later, the Westminster Amenity Societies Forum (WASF), a 20-strong group of residents' and environmental groups, issued an unprecedented hard-hitting condemnation of the Conservative Council in the form of a letter to all Councillors. In the letter, WASF Chairman Richard Cutts said residents and Councillors were routinely sidelined by a *"small number of people at the top of the council"* who prioritised the economy over the public interest. They claimed that *"futile consultations"* and *"unacceptable spin"* had led to a democratic void that had left residents without a voice.

Highlighting the Mound debacle, WASF commented, *"The mound appeared to emerge from a single consultant's suggestion that was then pushed forward by those running the Oxford Street District project. It has almost no support except from New West End Company and Marble Arch Bid. It was introduced at the spur of the moment by a few people at the top of the council."* The letter asked, *"This top-driven approach has proved to have failed… This very unfortunate outcome could have been avoided. Will this be the only debacle?"*

By now, the Council had rejected our call for an independent inquiry and had, instead, decided to mount an 'internal review' conducted by Council officers who had not been involved in the Mound decisions. We were sceptical that this would be sufficient to get to the bottom of what had happened and why, not least because the Council officers conducting the inquiry would, quite understandably, be thinking about their own future prospects at the Council when conducting their enquiries. Unsurprisingly, answers to our earlier questions were even more difficult to prize out of the Council, with the stock response that we would *"have to wait until the outcome of the internal review."*

The answers that we did get were generally unsatisfactory. First, the Council said that *"The Council's leadership weren't made aware of any concerns prior to opening."* This begged the question 'why not?', particularly as the Council Leader and Deputy Leader both visited the Mound prior to opening. The Council confirmed they were still working on a revised projection of future visitor numbers for when they would start to charge visitors again from September but admitted that the Council would generate significantly less in sponsorship than they previously projected. Significantly, they admitted that only one of the project's sponsors was under contract. Leader of the Labour Group Adam Hug said *"There is still a lot more that needs to be answered about what went wrong with the Council's decision making and project management on the Mound. The Council needs to be as open and transparent as possible if it wants to regain trust of residents before it spends £150m on the rest of the Oxford Street District project."*

Local reaction to the Mound continued to pour scorn on the Council, with the
'Marylebone Association Newsletter' of September 2021, commenting, *"The Marble Arch Mound's descent from "showpiece attraction" to public laughingstock has been fast*

and furious. Westminster had hoped that the Mound would bring accolades, but surely not the type that it is now regularly receiving, such as: "the worst thing that I've ever done in London ", and "'London's Worst Attraction"."

We were delighted to read the criticisms of the Conservatives' financial record which were set out clearly and succinctly by the Marylebone Association newsletter, *"Council Leader Rachael Robathan is on record as promising that "we will be able to cover almost all of the construction and operating costs over its six- month lifespan from ticket sales and sponsorship". However, the Council appears to be sufficiently embarrassed about the true costs involved to have refused to answer FOI requests. In addition, there will be no costs recovered from ticket sales as the decision has been made to permanently scrap charges for visiting the ill-fated attraction. The figure for sponsorship has been given at £450,000, but will Marks & Spencer, or other companies now want their names associated with a failed project?"*

The Council now faced a real choice. Should they try to 'close down' the bad news, or should they soldier on, hoping that the storm would blow itself out. They chose the latter and 'doubled down' on their support for the Mound, maintaining steadfastly that "doing nothing is not an option" if the Oxford Street retail area was to be revived. In reality, the Council had very little choice, with the Mound providing a massive looming public presence. We could not have been more pleased. The Mound would remain front and centre of our election campaign. The only issue we faced was to devise different ways of presenting the issues to continually repeat our political message that "it's time for change".

I was convinced that the '£6 Million Marble Arch Mound' would be a highly potent electoral issue. Within days it had 'cut through' with people from all shades of opinion, uniting Labour stalwarts and traditional Conservatives. Vitally, it was an issue that could not fail to influence 'floating voters'. As a veteran of Westminster's 1980's 'Homes for Votes' scandal, I could see that the 'Mound' was much more effective as a political 'game-changer'. While 'Homes for Votes' was clearly a disgraceful and illegal way to run the Council, the use of words like 'gerrymandering', and 'surcharge' were very much a 'niche' interest. In comparison, with the '£6 Million Mound' you needed no previous knowledge of local government or the law to understand the enormity of the Council's huge financial failure. But had it come too soon? Would we be able to keep the story in the public eye for the next nine months?

In September 2021, we presented a list of ways in which the £6 million could have been better spent by the Council. We pointed out that, for the past decade, the Conservatives had been making severe annual cuts to the Council's budget and telling residents from Paddington to Pimlico that services on which they depended were to be cut. We asked, *"what can you do with £6million?"* and presented a "menu" of what the Council could spend £6 million on:

- *Build 20 new homes for overcrowded families and those on the Council's housing waiting list; or*
- *Reinstate the massive cuts over the last decade to Westminster Council's children's play service, youth services and to children's centres; or*
- *Employ 30 extra newly qualified primary and secondary school teachers for the next five years; or*
- *Install solar panels on 500 blocks of flats in Westminster to address the climate emergency and cut energy bills for residents; or*
- *Fill 120,000 potholes in Westminster's roads; or*
- *Give a new computer to 20,000 primary, secondary and university students living in Westminster.*

In a letter to the *'Westminster Extra'*, I argued, *"Whatever you choose would be much, much, better than frittering away £6 million on this unforgiveable disaster. The Marble Arch Mound debacle should mark the end of an era for Westminster Conservatives."* As part of our communications strategy, we sent a letter every week to the *'Westminster Extra'* and invariably our letters were printed, giving us a regular public platform for direct and consistent message. Every Friday, Judith Southern picked copies of the *'Westminster Extra'* from the distribution bins in the area and delivered them to residents in the Star Street area. She became known locally by some people as the 'newspaper lady' and it certainly helped her get even better known.

Later that month, the Council revealed the £1,525,000 cost to the Council of scrapping entry charges to the Mound. We also castigated the Council for its failure to gather data on how many Mound visitors were combining a visit to the Mound with a shopping trip to Oxford Street or how much money was being spent in shops, pubs, cafés and restaurants as a result. We told the press, *"There was never any research undertaken to assess whether people would pay to visit the mound. Westminster Council has operated on the hope that "if you build it, they will come". However, that futile hope came from the Hollywood film 'Field of Dreams', not from real life. Now the Conservatives have finally accepted that no one will pay hard-earned money to visit what has been dubbed "the worst tourist attraction in London"."*

One of our central criticisms was that the promised 'panoramic vista' of Hyde Park and the rest of the West End never materialised. We asked, *"Why would anyone pay for "spectacular views" of McDonald's and the traffic on Park Lane and Edgware Road? As a result of the decision to make entry free, all of the predicted income will now be lost, adding to the loss to the council which will now be picked up by council taxpayers."* Our next letter to the 'Westminster Times' ended with a familiar question and message to residents, *"Can there by anything more damning of the Conservative's financial record than the £6 million Marble Arch Mound failure? For this reason alone, the Conservatives have no right to continue to mismanage the council's finances for a moment longer."*

Never short of ideas, our campaign was picking up pace and at the Council meeting on 22nd September we put down a motion calling for the Mound "to be put out of its misery" and pulled down. Our motion argued, *"That, as the Council has given up on trying to recover the cost of the Mound and it remains an international embarrassment to the city, steps are taken to dismantle and remove the Mound as soon as practicable."* Labour Group Leader Adam Hug told the Council meeting, *"The Mound project has been a major embarrassment to Westminster Council who have lost £6 million of taxpayers' money. It highlights the incompetence and arrogance of a Conservative administration that has been in power for far too long. It's time to get rid of the Conservatives and put the Mound out of its misery."* Unsurprisingly, whatever doubts some of the Conservative Group might have had about what the Mound was doing to their electoral chances, they all voted against our motion and it was defeated.

By the end of October 2021, the Council completed its 'internal review' of the Mound disaster with a report to the Scrutiny Committee making a series of damning findings. The review report revealed that, *"despite clear and repeated warnings",* the Mound was left unfinished when it opened in late July. The review report also found, *"There was a breakdown of project management of the Mound which, amongst other issues, led to confusion over roles and responsibilities, a lack of communication between staff and contractors working on different elements of the Marble Arch Mound project and a basic lack of project coordination and documentation."* The Council Chief Executive, Stuart Love, was forced to concede: *"The Council recognises that the project was not adequately scoped as a visitor attraction or a construction project at the outset. This subsequently led to a poor initial customer experience and an increase in costs, both of which are unacceptable"*

In more detail, the review report found three basic failures in the Council's management of the Mound project. *"There are three key reasons why the Mound opened too early and has run significantly over budget. These can broadly be summarised as (a) a failure of project management on the Marble Arch Mound project which meant risks were not effectively captured or escalated (b) project finances were mismanaged and misrepresented by the senior officers responsible for the Marble Arch Mound project and (c) a lack of effective governance, grip and oversight on the Marble Arch Mound project."*

On the question of costs, the review report revealed that a Cabinet Member Report (CMR) of 19th October 2021 admitted, *"Since May 2021 there have been a number of changes to the scope and design of the project, and this led to variations in the build and operation of the visitor attraction thereby impacting on the forecast cost."* The review report continued, *"Following the approval of the design, a number of changes were required during the construction of the Mound, particularly in relation to the extent and complexity of the scaffolding and sedum roof structure. As a consequence, the contract sum has increased to £4.5m."* We asked if these changes were approved? If so, by whom? If they were not approved, why not? Were Cabinet members informed of the 'changes to the scope and design of the project and their costs'? Did Cabinet members approve the changes and cost increases?

The project was riddled with flaws and oversights with the review report also revealing that, *"Furthermore, the full decommissioning of the site was not provided for in the original forecast. Whilst the original scope included an allowance for scaffold removal, it did not sufficiently reflect the scale or complexity of the decommissioning of the current structure, or an allowance for removing the sedum roof covering."* In addition, operator costs also increased. as the review report explained, *"The confidential appendix to the May 2021 CMR had included indicative figures for the operator* which ranged from £0.740m to £0.920m as the procurement process was not completed at that time. The winning tender was £0.793m but costs for the operator have now increased to £0.983m. The additional increase is due to necessary out-of-scope items not being included within the initial specification of the operator contract, for example welfare units and customer toilets, and additional security costs."

As for the promised £450,000 in sponsorship, the review report revealed that it had shrunk to about one third of the expected amount, *"The sponsorship agreements are in their final stage of development following close working with the sponsors to update the original agreements to fully reflect the offer of the Mound. Sponsorship funding received will be used to offset the overall cost of the project. The Council is expecting to receive £0.160m in sponsorship."*

Finally, for a Council which was usually so keen to publicise its every move, the review report unsurprisingly also revealed an additional £517,000 costs which *"primarily relate to branding and signage of the site, setting up of the internal space for the light exhibition, consultant fees, and utility services, which were not included in the original projections. These are essential to the operation of the Mound and benefit the customer experience."*

The Scrutiny Committee meeting itself was attended by Labour Group Leader Adam Hug. Despite our formal request for the Leader of the Council and Councillor Caplan to come to the meeting to answer questions, neither attended and all questions were answered by Council officers. The Committee heard how opportunities to rethink the scheme were missed in February when the design radically changed. There would no longer be a view down Oxford Street and the original plans to use soil, necessary to enable the vegetation promised in the glossy CGI promo pictures used until the Mound opened, were dropped in favour of using lower quality sedum, leaving plants 'dropping off' the Mound on the opening day.

The Scrutiny Committee heard how, once Councillor Caplan had urged officers to reduce costs, no Cabinet Member or Senior Officer asked how the cost savings were actually to be achieved. Essential infrastructure was temporarily taken out of the costings of the formally approved budget, only to be added in other ways after the project was given the final go ahead.

Senior officers also admitted that they had not visited the Mound since late June and the meeting heard that the Conservative Group of Councillors were the last to visit the Mound prior to opening, with a drinks party three days before the Mound opened to the public on 26th July. Surprisingly, no Councillor, Cabinet Member or senior officer who visited the site raised any concerns that things might be amiss. The Scrutiny Committee also confirmed that no Cabinet Member or senior officer checked that they were on track to meet their sponsorship targets.

Following the meeting Councillor Geoff Barraclough gave his comments, *"The council's Tory leadership are pinning the blame on a handful of rogue officers but there was a clear failure of culture from top to bottom. The project became a juggernaut that nobody was able to criticise. At least three opportunities to stop the Mound were missed as councillors and officers were dazzled by the CGI and failed to ask basic questions like "have you budgeted for toilets?"*

The review report and Scrutiny Committee demonstrated to a fault that Westminster suffered from a culture of complacency where basic questions were not asked, optimistic assumptions went unchallenged, mismanaged costs were not checked and everything was seen as rosy until the reviews came in. It showed how political expectations to 'operate at a quicker pace' led to corners being cut.

The monthly cost of keeping the Mound open was running at around £150,000, so there were loud cheers when the Council announced in mid-December 2021 that *"The Marble Arch*

Mound will close to the public on 9th January. The process of decommissioning the Mound will begin on 10th January, with the removal of the art installation and onsite operator facilities. Deconstruction of the Mound will then begin 18 January 2022 and our contractors FM Conway will erect a site perimeter barrier. It is anticipated that the decommissioning work will be completed around May 2022."

This sparked a further wave of media interest which we were happy to fuel. With the Mound expected to be around until election day on 5th May, everyone would have a constant reminder of the Conservatives' shameful blunders. And with the Mound on the doorstep of Hyde Park Ward, our local campaign would be able to use this visible evidence of Conservative incompetence in our conversations with residents. Keeping the issue alive in the media with new stories and new angles was our next challenge. We didn't have to wait long and just before Christmas a Council document detailing the Council's sponsorship efforts fell into our hands.

The Council's sponsorship 'prospectus' offered four levels of sponsorship for the Marble Arch Mound, which it called *"London's newest tourist attraction",*
- Lead Partner – £250,000 Contribution – *"Leader partners will be able to use the facility for multiple private hires and receive unlimited corporate access."*
- Official Partner – £100,000 Contribution – *"You will receive access for private hire and receive season tickets as well as discounted tickets for staff and partners."*
- Regional Partner – £50,000 Contribution *"You will be able to use the venue for two private hire events as well as receive access and discount benefits for staff."*
- Contribution Partner – £10,000 Contribution *"Suitable for organisations seeking to showcase their brand and utilise the venue for 1 private hire event."*

In May 2021, the Council's internal website boasted, *"This installation is the council's first venture into the visitor attraction world. It will have its own operations, ticketing system and merchandise in place to encourage people to visit the site".* Amongst the exaggerated claims made by the Council in its sponsorship prospectus about *"this innovative and iconic project"* which would give *"sweeping views of central London"* were:

"The installation introduces a park-like landscape of grass and trees and 'lifts' the corner of Hyde Park to create a spectacular 25-meter-tall viewpoint that gives visitors striking views of Oxford Street and the park, and a new perspective of Marble Arch itself."

"The striking presence of a new green mound will be visible from afar, drawing people to see it wherever they are in the area."

"When reaching the top, a viewing deck will offer 360-degrees views down Oxford Street and into Hyde Park, offering views never seen before by the wider public."

"Marble Arch Mound is expected to generate tens of millions of pounds in incremental spending for the local economy across the retail, hospitality and leisure sectors."

The Council also promised sponsors that, *"Your brand will be on display on one of London's most talked about attractions as visitors return to the city in large numbers this summer."* According to the Council's sponsorship prospectus, sponsors could also expect huge publicity for their involvement. *"Marble Arch Mound is a new London icon",* said the Council, *"We therefore expect it to receive significant media coverage both prior to its opening as well as throughout its operation in the summer months and leading to the Christmas period."* The Council certainly got this final prediction correct. The Marble Arch Mound was first on the *'Daily Mail's'* list of 'White Elephants of 2021'.

The '*Westminster Extra*' went to town with the story and our never-changing message. I told the press, *"The exaggerated claims the Council made about the Mound were never likely to be fulfilled and it is no surprise that sponsors were very difficult to find. Westminster Conservatives have yet again shown themselves to be very poor guardians of public money at a time when public services are being cut and when every penny counts to help the young, the elderly and others who are in need of assistance."*

The New Year brought another new revelation when we discovered that Elad Eisenstein, the Council's Oxford Street District Programme Director, responsible for the Mound fiasco, was paid £220,000 a year, making him the Council's highest paid employee, earning more than the Council's Chief Executive whose salary was £217,545 a year. The information was revealed in a Council document, '*Senior Salaries at Westminster Council, April 2021*', which set out details of 179 staff earning more than £68,000 a year and which the Council was obliged to publish each year under The Local Government Transparency Code, 2015. We also learned that the Oxford Street District Programme Director had resigned from the Council in the Autumn of 2021.

Determined to pin the blame on the Conservative leadership, I told the press, *"The Leader of the Council needs to explain why she signed off such an enormous salary. The Conservative Councillors responsible for the Marble Arch Mound should hang their heads in shame and apologise to the people of Westminster for wasting so much public money."* And, of course, I finished with our 'signature' message to residents, *"Westminster residents will have their opportunity to pass judgment on Boris Johnson's Conservatives in May when all Councillors will be up for election and when Labour will be putting forward a positive and practical agenda for improving public services and ending the current Conservative financial incompetence."*

The growing unpopularity of Prime Minister Boris Johnson encouraged us to link national and local politics and to introduce the phrase 'Boris Johnson's Conservatives' into our regular communications.

Later in January we continued our assault by demonstrating how the Council got its figures wrong on the impact that the Mound would have on the Oxford Street economy. If you recall, the Council justified building the Mound by claiming that the 280,000 expected visitors would boost Oxford Street shops. So, we laid out the facts, simply and clearly. It goes like this,

- 600,000 people visit Oxford Street every day
- This works out at more than 4 million people visiting Oxford Street each week
- In all, over 200 million people visit Oxford Street every year
- This means that the Conservatives have spent £6 million attracting less than half of one day's total number of visitors to Oxford Street

I made the point that, in terms of economic impact, this was just 'a drop in the ocean' and visitors to the £6m Marble Arch Mound have had absolutely no effect on the success of any of the businesses along Oxford Street. I told the press, *"If the Conservatives had wanted to attract shoppers back to Oxford Street they would have been better giving 250,000 Westminster residents a voucher for £24 to spend in Oxford Street's shops, cafes or bars."*

At the end of January 2022, we 'refreshed' the Mound story by reflecting on the Conservatives' 'Top 10' key failures:

1. It cost a staggering £6million – triple the £2million set aside for the project
2. The Council's Deputy Leader resigned following the massive budget overspend

3. Reviews for the 82ft mound of scaffolding were so bad that the Council was forced to scrap the £8 entrance fee out of embarrassment.
4. The Mound was branded the 'London's worst tourist attraction' and a 'waste of money' following six months of mockery and ridicule, making Westminster an "international laughing-stock".
5. Much of the view into neighbouring Hyde Park was obstructed by trees.
6. The Westminster Council official in charge of the Mound fiasco was paid more than the authority's Chief Executive with a £220,000 salary, making him the authority's highest-paid employee.
7. Marble Arch Mound was visited 250,000 times – less than half a day's footfall on Oxford Street and therefore making a miniscule contribution to the local economy
8. It cost the Council £150,000 a month to keep the Mound open, after it refused to listen to Labour's calls to 'put the Mound out of its misery' and pull it down.
9. In October 2021, a Council internal investigation of the Mound project described the soaring costs of the scheme as "devastating" and "avoidable".
10. The report by the Council's Chief Executive said there were "clear and repeated warnings" about the project being overbudget.

Our 'Top 10' Conservative failures press release was followed by an unexpected intervention by the Mound architects, Dutch firm MVRDV, who issued an impassioned defence of their position on the company's website on 28th January 2022. MVRDV blasted Westminster Conservatives for their failures in controlling costs, poor construction and ignoring warnings. *"As a practice, we have rarely seen such a loveless execution of our designs,"* they say. In their website article they said they *"wish to provide our account of the events, while also critically examining our role in this and publicly acknowledging our mistakes."*

On costs, the MVRDV said, *"The cost of the whole project would be £1.25 million, of which 0.8 percent, £10,000, was set aside for the design."* There was a catalogue of construction failures, *"The sedum on the hillside had dried out in places, appearing as though it hadn't been watered in months. Some of it dried up during the week of intense summer heat ......It was never replaced. Some planting ......was not completed at all, with the sad low point being on the west side, where plastic sheeting offered a pitiful stand-in, as if we'd run out of plants."* The article continued to fan the flames, *"The elevator at the crest of the mound was unfinished and stuck out like a sore thumb above the hill. The vegetation's irrigation system was flawed, spilling water into the street....... The overall impression of it was that it had been left to rot in the middle of London's most important shopping district."*

In their most damning passage, MVRDV stuck the knife in deep, *"When we were finally able to travel and see the project for ourselves, the deception was obvious: there had been virtually no maintenance, making the waste of money complete. What should have been a celebration of London became a loveless installation that, with a few nice green plants here and there, provides a glimpse of what might have been. In our thirty years of practice, MVRDV has never before experienced such nonchalance and laxity with our design work."*

The Council project management failures were laid bare, *"WCC commissioned FM Conway to realise the project and then barely looked at it again..... Through a mixture of budget constraints and a lack of communication, many details concerning the mound's construction were decided without our involvement..... and frequent communication efforts from our side toward WCC were increasingly ignored."*

MVRDV's intervention sparked further questions about the inadequacy of the Council's internal enquiry. I asked why the Council's internal report *"failed to pick up any of MVRDV's first-hand experience of this financial and construction fiasco.*

Why did costs escalate so wildly? Why was the execution of the project such an unmitigated disaster? Why were warnings about the premature opening ignored?"

Keeping up the weekly 'revelations' in the *'Westminster Extra'* was no easy task and required regular re-hashing of previous stories. In the run-up to the Council budget making meeting in late February we released details of the 'Price of the Conservatives' £6m Marble Arch Mound Fiasco'. I had been at pains to stress to my colleagues that in all our publicity, that we did not simply call it the 'Marble Arch Mound', but to cover it in its full glory as the *'£6 Million Marble Arch Mound'* so that the massive scale of the financial cost would be at the very top of the agenda. So, with some creative license, we revealed that £6m Marble Arch Mound financial mismanagement was responsible for,

- Council rents going up £5 a week, so as to bring in £3m extra income.
- Parking charges going up, too, raising £1m extra income.
- Adult Social Services are being cut by £500,000 and
- Mayfair Library being under threat of closure to save £200,000 a year in rent.

We told residents, *"All this could have been avoided if the Conservatives had not wasted £6 million of your money on the Marble Arch Mound disaster. These increased charges, social service cuts and library closures affect everyone in Westminster, whether you live in Paddington or Pimlico, whether you are rich or poor, young or old. The £6 million Marble Arch Mound sums up everything that is wrong about Boris Johnson's Westminster Council – world-class wasters of your money."*

A few weeks' later we re-packaged our list of things the Council could have done with £6 million. We argued, *"According to Crisis, it costs £1,426 to successfully help a* homeless person off the streets. For £6 million, Westminster Council could have helped over 4,200 people off the streets. It costs £50 to fill a pothole in the road. For £6 million, Westminster Council could have filled 120,000 potholes in Westminster's roads. A new laptop computer costs £300. For £6 million, Westminster Council could have given a new computer to 20,000 primary, secondary and university students living in Westminster." We compared this to the Mound 'facts and figures', *"Instead, we got a useless Mound which attracted less than 1,400 people a day on average, even though it was free for the six months it was open. The footfall generated by 1,400 people would not register anything meaningful on Oxford Street retailers' tills."*

By March, two months before the Council elections, we were desperate to keep the Mound stories running. We released details of the Mound demolition costs, which added up to £660,000, and were included in the £6 million bill. Two days before the election we were able to reveal that the Council's 'Community Contribution', which collected voluntary donations from wealthy residents living in Council Tax band H properties, had plummeted by 68% in 2021. Under the scheme, the donated money goes to charity, helping young people, rough sleepers and tackling loneliness in old age.

In the three years, 2018-2020 the City of Westminster Charitable Trust received £1,103,720 in income, In the pandemic year of 2020-21, a record £512,000 was raised. But the figures for 2021-22 showed only £161,700 had been contributed, a 68% fall in one year. Crucially, the invitation to contribute to the fund went out days after the Council announced plans for the Marble Arch Mound. Labour's finance spokesperson Councillor David Boothroyd said, *"When Boris Johnson's Westminster Conservatives waste money, it's local people who suffer. Who would voluntarily give money to such a spendthrift council? Now it seems wasting money on the Mound means less money given to help local young people, elderly and rough sleepers."*

For over a year, the '£6 Million Marble Arch Mound' sustained and fed our election campaign, giving it purpose, strength and focus. We had managed to keep it going week-after-week, month-after-month, by repeating it ad nauseum. I had no doubt that this was the best strategy, remembering *'Sunday Times'* editor Harold Evans' advice to his staff when campaigning on the thalidomide scandal in the 1960's. *"When you are fed up with repeating the same stories with the same arguments,"* he told his reporters, *"that's the first time most people will have read about it"*.

But, at the same time, we also knew that the Mound scandal alone would not be enough to win the marginal wards. We had to put in the work right across Westminster in the Wards that would win us extra seats we needed for victory.

Chapter 5 – All Politics is Local

It was the father of former Speaker of the US House of Representatives, Thomas 'Tip' 'O'Neill who coined the famous phrase 'All Politics is Local'. His son had lost a 'safe' Congressional district by campaigning on foreign policy issues, while his successful Republican opponent concentrated on basic everyday concerns. 'Tip' O'Neill soon learned his lesson and won the seat back at the next election with a laser-sharp attention to the concerns of the residents of Cambridge, Massachusetts.

Similarly, in the UK, Frank Dobson MP would regularly tell the tale of canvassing on St Pancras housing estates with Lena Jeger MP. Knocking on residents' doors, Lena Jeger would announce, *"I am your Labour MP and I am campaigning to end nuclear proliferation, will you sign our petition?"* On one occasion, an angry woman responded, *"Don't talk to me about nuclear proliferation, what are you going to do to stop them p***ing in the lift?"* *"That's a Council matter, not something for an MP,"* Jeger replied. *"Well, if you can't stop them p***ing in the lift, you're not going to get very far ending nuclear proliferation!"*, retorted the woman.

More recently, writing in *'The New Yorker'* in October 2022, Nicholas Lemann, described how the US Democrats were winning back marginal areas through their 'aggressive mundaneness' campaigns in 'swing' states like Nevada and New Hampshire. *"What they are trying to do,"* explains Lemann, *"is establish a reputation as super-practical, non-moralistic, not very partisan, and intent on improving the everyday circumstances of people's lives."* Lemann continues, *"It comes from a reading of American politics right now as an open competition for the loyalties of voters who aren't especially affluent and who don't feel especially secure or in control of their circumstances."*

Concluding his analysis of the Democrat strategy, Lehmann argues, *"The Democrats are pitching the idea that they will make your life better in tangible, concrete ways: they'll improve your kids' schools, they'll keep you safe, they'll protect you from disastrous health-care crises, and they'll try to make sure that you have a good job, while the Republicans are busy enacting a drama of cultural grievance."* My observation is that this analysis also crosses the Atlantic and applies very much to UK politics, too.

****

Our campaigns in Westminster followed the 'All Politics is Local' approach to the letter, none more so than in Bayswater Ward where we hoped to build on Maggie Carman's successful 2018 campaign by winning the other two seats. Since 2018, Maggie had built up very strong support and a formidable local reputation by holding regular advice surgeries and taking up huge amounts of housing and other casework. I worked with her to send out a monthly email *'Bayswater & Lancaster Gate Labour Action Report'* to an ever-growing list of subscribers, detailing the impressive list of issues she was dealing with and getting practical results for residents. Combined with regular newsletter deliveries, the Labour presence in Bayswater Ward was constant.

Supported by Max Sullivan, one of Maggie's unsuccessful running mates in 2018 who went on to Chair Westminster North Labour Party, and James Small-Edwards, a young member working for a Labour MP, the Bayswater campaign gathered around it a core of regular doorknockers and leaflet-deliverers. Maggie and her team were relentless in taking up local issues. In March 2021, Maggie wrote to the Council to urge action to stop engine idling by lorries on Bishop's Bridge Road servicing the Whiteley's redevelopment after residents wrote to her to say, *"I have complained both to the traffic marshal and the drivers and reactions have been either abusive or just patronising. Sometimes there are as many as 10 lorries and all are diesel and all seem to think it's OK to do* this. There are families living on both sides of the road and schools and nurseries nearby."

Later that month Maggie called for action on Artesian Road rubbish dumping after residents got in touch to complain, *"The daily abuse of our streets and immediate neighbourhood continues. Most recently, I have reported the same – and growing – accumulation of rubbish around the overflowing 'big, black bins' on Artesian Road, outside the Church of St Mary of the Angels three times."*

This was followed by Maggie calling on BT to stop the phone boxes on Bishops Bridge Road being used by sex workers to advertise their services, by blocking the phone numbers advertised on the postcards, regularly removing the advertising cards and cleaning the phone boxes more regularly.

A much bigger issue arose in May 2021 when it was revealed that there were plans to sell the gardens in Prince's Square for over £5 million, which might see the gardens no longer open to the 300 local residents who currently used them. There were fears that the garden might become an oligarch's private garden or be turned into a venue for noisy functions and corporate events. Maggie contacted residents and led the call to the Council to support the residents' legal fight to continue to be able to use the square in the future. Maggie said, *"It is important to recognise the careful stewardship, hours of voluntary work and generous donations by Prince's Square residents that have made this beautifully landscaped and well preserved central London square that the owners are now trying to profit from."*

Under pressure from Maggie and residents, who now formed the 'Friends of Prince's Square Gardens' group, the estate agents handling the sale had to amend the particulars, asking bidders to *"please specify how you intend to use, manage and preserve the Garden following completion and how you would propose to allow local residents to have access to the*

Gardens." Maggie also helped residents to make an application to have Prince's Square Gardens designated as an Asset of Community Value, which would give residents more time to work on their proposals and provide other safeguards. Maggie told the local press, *"I will keep fighting alongside local residents to protect their rights to use Prince's Square Gardens. I urge the owners to see sense and come to a settlement that puts residents in control, but whoever owns the site they must protect the rights of local people."*

With over 2,000 families in temporary accommodation, housing issues were at the top of our concerns and in June 2021, the Bayswater and Lancaster Gate Labour Action Team campaigned against development plans that failed to provide the number of affordable housing units as laid down by the Council's City Plan. The development in Queensway comprised the construction of 61 flats, with just 8 flats at intermediate rents. This fell well below the requirement of the City Plan which would see 24 affordable homes (a mixture of social and intermediate). We also pointed out that the developer involved had previously donated £50,000 to the Conservative Party from an address in the British Virgin Islands.

In November 2021, Maggie urged the Council to reopen the lower ground floor of Paddington Library after a resident told her, *"I was disappointed to find that the lower ground floor of Paddington is still closed and the non-fiction books are still unavailable. The librarian at the desk told me that there's no definite date for its return and that I should take it up with the council. Apparently, there is a problem with black mould, and an unwillingness for Westminster to meet the cost of removal."* It was interesting that the Mound was beginning to be the 'example of choice' when residents wanted to describe the Council's wastefulness. *"It seems absurd that a Council that can, notoriously, spend £6 million on a hill, is unable to re-open its own libraries"*, commented the resident.

The Bayswater and Lancaster Gate Labour Action Teams worked very closely, not least because the Ward boundary changes had shifted many voters from Ward to another. The Lancaster Gate Labour candidates - Ellie Ormsby, Ryan Jude and Dario Goodwin - knew they had an uphill task, but we ensured that they received the support of experienced campaigners Andy Whitley and Connor Jones from the start and right through the campaign. A typical Saturday and Sunday campaign day would see the candidates from both Wards in one of the Wards in the morning and in the other Ward in the afternoon.

A big issue for Lancaster Gate and Bayswater residents was the noise and disruption from the massive Whiteley's redevelopment project on Queensway. Whiteley's department store had been a fixture on Queensway since Victorian times. A major regeneration project in the 1980s gave the building a rebirth - until the opening of Westfield at White City in Shepherd's Bush shifted retail spending habits further west. The new owners decided that the future of the Whiteley's building required an almost total demolition, leaving the façade as the only reminder of the glory days of the past. For local residents, this meant years of noise, disruption and dust.

The very least that residents might have expected was for their local Council to protect them from the worst of this daily intrusion into their lives. But, not so, as a Freedom of Information (FoI) request by Lancaster Gate Labour Candidate, Ellie Ormsby revealed. Ellie discovered that, over the previous year, Westminster Council granted the Whiteley's contractors near daily permissions to operate beyond their agreed working hours (8am-6pm weekdays, 8am-1pm Saturdays only).

The FoI request revealed that, out of the 76 applications to work beyond their core hours sent to the Council in the previous year, not one was rejected. With each application often covering a period of days, if not weeks, in 2021 the contractors had permission to work beyond the agreed working hours on over 300 days. This effectively rendered the permitted working hours agreement redundant, with deliveries starting at 6:30am and, in extreme cases, works permitted to go on until 11pm.

With near constant noise from industrial machinery and vibrations from the incoming heavy vehicles, this rendered many residents' lives a misery and homes unliveable. Ellie Ormsby said, *"The noise and disruption from this development has been awful for residents in Lancaster Gate, not to mention the pollution and dust. Residents were promised window cleaning over a year ago as compensation for the damage by the developers, but this has yet to materialise. Local people deserve better."* Councillor Maggie Carman made an even more telling point, *"During the previous phase of drilling out, residents from across Bayswater told me how their lives were made a misery by months of unbearable noise and vibrations. The response to our complaints was to ban us from resident engagement meetings."*

Perhaps, Maggie Carman's most famous victory came, appropriately, in April 2022, just a few days before the Council elections when the Ma Dame nightclub in Porchester Road lost its licence. It was a fantastic victory for long suffering residents of Westbourne Park Road, Porchester Road and Celbridge Mews when the nightclub lost its licence in a tense hearing at a special Licensing Committee Review at City Hall. For years residents had been plagued by noisy revellers leaving the club in the early hours of the morning, shouting, slamming car doors and carrying on partying. One long-time resident recounted how he had been assaulted while trying to film evidence. The Licencing panel also heard how other residents, whose homes shared a party wall with Ma Dame, were reduced to leaving their homes at the weekend to escape the incessant noise. The panel were shown some shocking images of defecation, urination and vomit in the Mews along with videos of rowdy behaviour and drug use.

Maggie had worked closely over the years with local residents to call for the licence to be reviewed. Residents were sick to death of their complaints being ignored and were at a loss to understand how the club's owner, given the deeply concerning issues raised at the hearing, was allowed to continue running the club for so long. Echoing the thoughts of many, one resident told Maggie, *"Amazing result! It's been a long journey and you've been with us all the way."*

****

Concentrating on the 'target' Wards did not mean we abandoned the 'safe' Labour Wards. Indeed, with Karen Buck as the Member of Parliament for Westminster North there has been constant attention to the everyday needs of her 60,000 plus constituents every day, 365 days of the year for over a quarter of a century. The staff at Karen's constituency office in Shirland Mews, North Paddington, work tirelessly fielding hundreds of emails, telephone calls and letters a day. Karen deals with many of the enquiries herself, badgering Council officials, contacting housing association staff and writing to Government Ministers and their departments and agencies to sort out housing, education, immigration, nationality, benefits and numerous other problems that beset some of the most vulnerable people.

Karen has been an inspiration to everyone in Westminster North for over 30 years, both as our Member of Parliament and previously as a Councillor for Queen's Park Ward. In addition, she is a leading Parliamentarian campaigning on a wide range of social, housing and humanitarian causes. Few people can match her commitment and energy. She is invariably at every weekend canvassing session, come rain, come shine, knocking on doors, delivering leaflets and talking to grateful residents in every ward in Westminster North.

A common experience for canvassers at election time when calling on residents was to be greeted with a smile when you announced that you were calling on behalf of Karen Buck, the

Labour Candidate. The smiles would invariably be followed by, *"Yes, I'm voting for Karen, she has helped me"*. It was Karen's genuine record of achievement that underpinned our campaigns in Bayswater, Lancaster Gate and Little Venice Wards, as well as those already represented by Labour Councillors.

In Church Street Ward, for example, Labour Councillors Aicha Less, Matt Noble and Aziz Toki were kept very busy by the many residents living in Council flats on the Lisson Green and Church Street Estates. With a regular advice surgery at Church Street Library, Councillors had a very full local caseload that could not be ignored and required close attention. In addition, they led local campaigns to get improvements in the area. The same was true for Labour Councillors representing Harrow Road, Westbourne and Queen's Park Wards (including myself as a Queen's Park Councillor where I made sure I prioritised case work from my constituents).

In March 2021, after a long campaign from residents, local groups and Church Street Councillors, the Council finally installed a zebra crossing on Rossmore Road. Residents living on the Lisson Green and the Blandford Estates benefitted from these pedestrian safety improvements. Later, in September 2021, Councillor Matt Noble presented a petition from over 100 Lisson Green residents to the Council calling on the Council to return the Greenside Hall back to community use after 18 months as a Covid test centre. Residents said in their petition, *"In 2020 it made perfect sense to turn our Greenside community centre into a Covid test centre: there was great need to get tested locally and staff had to work from home anyway. However, with many more home test kits available now the centre is near-deserted and dead silent. This at a time when people are allowed to socialise again. We need Greenside Hall back to serve us once again as a community centre."*

And with 38% of anti-social behaviour (ASB) complaints in Westminster Housing coming from Church Street, Westbourne and Queens Park wards it was no surprise that in January 2022, Church Street Councillors called for strong action to tackle anti-social behaviour. Councillor Aisha Less told the Council meeting, *"Anti-social behaviour is often downplayed as a petty, 'low-level' crime. But put yourself in their shoes – to suffer from ASB is an ordeal that causes misery, disturbs sleep, anxiety, work, and relationships – leaving victims feeling unsafe and afraid in their own homes. It can feel like you are living a nightmare."*

It was important to keep to 'business as usual' in Queen's Park, not least to support our new candidate, Cara Sanquest, who had been selected to take my place. We had a 'walkabout' across the Ward in the Summer of 2021 when I briefed her on some of the issues we had dealt with over the years and introduced her to residents as we walked through the Avenues. I also ensured that the monthly email *'Queen's Park Ward Labour Action Reports'* included details of all the local campaigns and everyday issues we were taking up.

I kept campaigning on some of the issues I had been dealing with over previous 25 years. In April 2021, I congratulated our City Inspectors, Nuno and Hussein, who arranged to remove graffiti on the walls at the Ha' Penny Steps bridge across the canal along the Harrow Road and remove items from the latest dredge of the canal. I followed this up later in the year by calling on the Council to encourage 'community gardening' to deter rubbish dumping at the bases of trees. I argued that allowing residents to plant and take care of the shrubs and plants would reduce rubbish dumping. I pointed to the evidence from a number of streets in the area where, not only was there much less dumping, but the streets looked brighter and 'cared for'.

Closer to the election, in March 2022, we were successful in persuading the Council's Waste Team to issue residents in Ilbert Street with three new bins – for general waste, for food recycling and for general recycling – as part of a pilot scheme to keep rubbish off the streets and increase recycling. This was following a decision we took to move two sets of Big Black Waste and Recycling Bins from Ilbert Street which were attracting dumped furniture, mattresses, fridges and more on a daily basis. Most of the dumping we believed came from landlords clearing flats or from builders. The Big Black Bins were used mostly by Ilbert Street residents, so the three new waste bins provided enough capacity for their waste and recycling. It was very gratifying to get very positive responses from residents, both about their new bins and the end to dumping along Ilbert Street.

Improvements often take a long time to deliver and I was very pleased to see that a new zebra crossing had finally been installed outside St Luke's Primary School on Fernhead Road. We had been campaigning for the new zebra crossing for many years and even when it was finally agreed it took an age for the work to start and be completed. The new zebra crossing has made it much safer to cross the road between the school and the Saltram Crescent area, as well as slowing down the traffic on this very busy road. It was a great to see it finally delivered.

****

Even though we won all three seats in Maida Vale ward in 2018, we were taking no chances as the battle with the Conservatives had always been hard-fought. Rita Begum, who had first won a Maida Vale seat from the Conservatives in 2014, was stepping down and she was replaced by Iman Less. Both Geoff Barraclough and Nafsika Butler-Thalassis had developed strong links with residents since 2018 with regular campaigns on local issues which they continued with added vigour during 2021 and 2022.

A key strength of the Maida Vale campaign was that Geoff, Nafsika, Rita and Iman also took up issues beyond the remit of the Council, as well as those affecting Council services.

They represented residents' concerns across the board, including concerns in March 2021, that the Randolph Surgery GP Practice was sold to a US healthcare giant without any consultation or notice given to patients. The Councillors organised a petition demanding an explanation from the Central London and North-West London Clinical Commissioning Groups about how the sale was allowed to happen. The petition explained:

"When a GP practice changes ownership, the contract is normally handed back to the relevant Clinical Commissioning Group (CCG) which then starts the process of finding a different company to run the practice. This happened in 2019 at the Randolph Surgery when the contract was given to AT Medics, with the full participation of the patient reference group. This time however, AT Medics has been acquired by a business called Operose Ltd which is a subsidiary of the $35 billion Centene Corporation based in St Louis, Missouri. This manoeuvre allows Centene to avoid a procurement process or any public scrutiny."

Nafsika wrote to North-West London CCG to ask them to clarify how the sale could be done without any patient consultation or even notice to the patients directly affected. *"Whatever legal loophole may have been found in this case,"* she said, *"the way this has been handled goes against the principles of 'No decision about me without me'. People have a right to know which organisation provides their care and has access to their data and medical records. They are not supposed to find out from the news."*

Planning issues were a very hot topic of local concern, and in April 2021, the Maida Vale councillors welcomed the Planning Committee decision to refuse permission for a basement conversion at Wymering Mansions. The new flat proposed for undeveloped storage units and a "crawl space" beneath the block would have had low ceilings, little natural light and no access for wheelchairs or mobility scooters. Worse, the new flat would only be accessible via a 50m walk through a narrow gate and through the garden at the rear of the block. The London Fire Brigade objected saying the challenging location would delay attendance if the flat caught fire. Councillor Geoff Barraclough, spoke on behalf of concerned neighbours at the Planning Committee meeting, commenting, *"This proposed flat provides sub-standard and dangerous accommodation. In three years on the Planning Committee, I've never seen a worse design."*

On Monday 12th July 2021, disaster struck Maida Vale Ward when heavy rainfall caused serious flooding on Kilburn Park Road and Shirland Road in Maida Vale leaving dozens of basement flats uninhabitable. Flood water rising from the sewers reached as high as three feet in some homes. Residents' furniture and bedding was ruined and many treasured possessions destroyed. This came despite a £17m flood prevention scheme by Thames Water which built two giant reservoirs, at Westbourne Green and Tamplin Gardens, specifically to contain the risk of sewer flooding.

Councillor Geoff Barraclough was on the scene immediately to help residents and to get the Council emergency team down on site. *"It was heart-breaking to see residents piling their water-logged possessions in the street."* he said. *"In the short-term we have been in touch with Westminster Housing and Notting Hill Genesis demanding action to help their tenants cope with the damage and disruption. Longer term, we need answers about how this was allowed to happen. It's clear that the expensive new flood defences failed and we need to know why. This can't be allowed to happen again."*

Within a few days the Maida Vale and Harrow Road Ward Councillors launched a crowd-funding campaign for flood relief efforts with 'One Westminster', the local voluntary organisation 'umbrella' group. Over one hundred basement flats had been flooded, with water rising up to three feet deep in many peoples' homes within minutes. The water was heavily polluted with sewage and everything it touched – bedding, furniture, white goods etc – had to be thrown away. Most of the affected families were social housing tenants and many could not afford insurance. Many were older or vulnerable residents who didn't have the capacity to deal with this level of devastation. All monies raised were used to support to residents in replacing items or costs incurred due to the floods.

The following week the Maida Vale Councillors continued their call for extra help for flooding victims, calling on Westminster Council to make two gestures of support to residents. On Council Tax, they asked the Council to exempt the flooded properties from Council Tax while they are uninhabited. And on parking charges, they asked the Council to exempt builders and other tradespeople working on the flats from parking charges (£25.50 per day) and from skip hire fees (£81).

Speaking up for residents, Nafsika said, *"It's not fair that people still have to pay Council Tax when they can't live in their flats. Westminster should show some solidarity with its residents and make an exemption."* While Geoff argued, *"Parking charges are significant. It would be a welcome signal of support for the hard-pressed flood victims to exempt their contractors from trades parking and skip permit fees."*

The flooding problems were to run for many more months, giving the Maida Vale Councillors further cause to battle on behalf of residents. In addition, new issues emerged. In October 2021, the Maida Vale Councillors called for action on the derelict Carlton Dene site on Carlton Vale where the Council had plans to develop an Extra Care facility for older residents, along with a new affordable housing block. The closure of Carlton Dene and the demolition of Peebles House next door were signed-off in 2019, yet development work was not planned to begin until mid-2022 at the earliest. Apparently, the Council had difficulties finding a private operator to build and manage the new facility. Meanwhile, the empty buildings lay derelict and had attracted squatters and weeds in equal measure. *"These buildings could still be in use but, instead, are an eyesore that is attracting anti-social behaviour. Westminster needs to speed up its development plans and get on with the job,"* said Geoff Barraclough.

Traffic issues also gave the Maida Vale team the opportunity to speak up for local residents and to get practical improvements to improve road safety. In November 2021, the Maida Vale Labour councillors launched a petition asking Westminster Council to take action against speeding motorists on Lauderdale Road. Lauderdale Road is a broad street with one-way traffic. Most car drivers obeyed the 20mph limit, but a significant minority treated it like a racetrack. Residents were very worried about the risk of accidents and called for traffic calming measures be put in place. In the same month, the Maida Vale Councillors started another petition asking Westminster Council to commission a study on redesigning the Shirland Road junction to minimise congestion, improve air quality and maximise the safety of people on foot and bicycles. Shirland Road is a busy through route where it meets Kilburn Park Road, Chippenham Road and Malvern Road and where cars, buses, cyclists and pedestrians all converge on a small area. Councillor Nafsika Butler-Thalassis told the local press, *"There is a particular problem with the zebra crossing on Kilburn Park Road. Traffic frequently stops on the crossing as it waits to turn into Shirland Road. This blocks people on foot and forces them to dodge, unsafely, around the stationary cars and buses."*

In December, the Maida Vale Team launched yet another petition, this time about the threat posed to the Bakerloo Line following the pandemic and loss of income for Transport for London (TfL). Transport for London depends heavily on fare income and this fell dramatically since the start of the Covid pandemic. Unlike the national rail services, TfL only had short term help from the Government and now the situation had become so serious that closing an entire tube line was being considered, with the Bakerloo seen as most at risk. The petition, which we posted on the Labour Group website and included in the regular monthly 'Action Report' email, argued,

"We are critically dependent on the Bakerloo line to get around the rest of London from our homes, to work and to leisure and to meet our friends and family. We also rely on public transport as a major contributor to tackling pollution and reducing carbon emissions."

The Maida Vale Team started 2022 with a campaign to 'Save the Monkey Bars' in Paddington Recreation Ground, calling on the Council to rethink plans to replace a much-used set of monkey bars with a large "smart activator" digital screen. The new screen would be used to run pre-recorded exercise classes. As a parent with young children, Councillor Nafsika Butler-Thalassis said, *"My daughter and her friends love these monkey bars. I don't see why this digital screen needs to take their place. Let's put it in a different part of the park and see whether it actually helps people exercise before we tear down well-loved equipment we know works."*

In February the Maida Vale Labour councillors returned to the vacant Peebles House flats and called on them to be used for temporary accommodation. This block of nine flats had been empty for over two years and was attracting graffiti and fly tipping. Tenants were moved out of Peebles House in 2019 but three years later no work had yet begun. *"Residents must be wondering why the Council insisted that they move out in such a hurry in 2019,"* said Geoff Barraclough. *"The site is overgrown and covered with graffiti. Why not re-open Peebles House for temporary accommodation until the Carlton Dene project finally begins?"*

Finally, saving the best campaign result to the last, just weeks before the election, the Maida Vale Labour Councillors were able to claim that they had saved £141,000 for over-charged leaseholders. In April 2022, following pressure from the Maida Vale Councillors, Westminster Council admitted making a mistake when issuing service charge demands to leaseholders at four blocks on the Maida Vale estate. The total amount over-charged was £141,437 across 116 properties, an average of £1,219 for each flat.

The Maida Vale Councillors successfully challenged the annual bills which had risen by over 80% to a massive £3,200 for a typical flat. Costs for cleaning and grounds maintenance had tripled over the previous year. Many leaseholders had been worried about how they would pay the charges at the same time as other bills are going up so fast.

In response to the Maida Vale councillors, Westminster Housing Department admitted making *"a charging error for the following service charge categories; block cleaning, co-op repairs, grounds maintenance and window cleaning."* As a result, all leaseholders in Thurso, Atholl, Braemer and Dundee Houses were sent revised bills with annual charges, on average, £1,219 lower than before. Councillor Geoff Barraclough told the local press, *"Leaseholders will be very relieved to get the new, lower bills but we are worried that Westminster's systems generated these mistakes in the first place. If your service charges rise unexpectedly, challenge them. Don't suffer in silence."* Councillor Nafsika Butler-Thalassis added, *"I don't think Westminster Council realises the distress these bills caused. People are struggling with inflation on all sides and the last thing they need is mistakes like this."*

Going into an election having won over £1,000 for a significant number of residents was a great way for the Maida Vale Team to end the campaign and fitting result for four years of hard work.

****

The campaign in Pimlico South was a great deal more problematic. Not only had the Ward boundaries been changed to bring in the 1,100 apartment Dolphin Square building, but the strong Labour-voting Peabody and Ebury Bridge Estates were also transferred out of the Ward and into next door

Knightsbridge & Belgravia Ward. On top of this, the existing Churchill Ward was split, with two Labour Councillors (Andrea Mann and Shamin Talukder) and one Conservative (who had defected from Labour in 2016 following Jeremy Corbyn's election as Labour leader).

A further complication arose in May 2021, when one of the Churchill Labour Councillors, Andrea Mann, resigned for personal reasons. Andrea had been a very active and effective campaigner in Churchill Ward and we were very sorry to see her leave. However, 'as one door closes, another one opens', and Andrea's departure paved the way for Liza Begum to take her place. Liza (who is Shamim's sister) had already cut her teeth in the local campaign to ensure that Walden House residents (of which she was one) were rehoused locally by the Council as part of a proposed development by The Grosvenor Estate. Liza had mobilised Walden House residents and the Grosvenor tenants in the adjacent Cundy House to take on the might of the Duke of Westminster. And she won, forcing both the Council and Grosvenor to revise their previous plans to rehouse Walden House residents across the borough. The revised plans required Grosvenor to build new social housing as part of the new development so that Walden House tenants could be rehoused on site.

The Churchill Ward by-election on 6th May 2021, also gave us the opportunity to update and improve our local contacts with residents and upgrade our local election campaign 'machinery'. We were delighted when Liza, who was particularly effective speaking to residents on the doorstep, romped home with an increased majority of 324 votes. The result was:

Liza Begum, Labour: 1,340
Conservative: 1,016
Liberal Democrat: 295
Green Party: 186

Notwithstanding the excellent by-election result, we were taking nothing for granted, and Liza was soon pitched into a long-running battle about the Council's proposed redevelopment of Darwin House and the derelict 'Balmoral Castle' pub on the Churchill Gardens Estate. The redevelopment proposals had been around for many years and had split the local community. Some residents were particularly worried about the impact of the proposed design on neighbouring residents, the lack of social housing, problems around accessing the site during construction and the impact on local parking. In a letter to the Planning Officer, Liza and Shamim wrote:

"Churchill Gardens Estate is a conservation area with Grade II listed landscaping, so it is important that the Council gets the scheme right. We are concerned that the current design of the development is not in keeping with the design of the estate and would result in a major loss of privacy and light to residents living in the surrounding blocks, particularly for those in Maitland House, Shelley House and the riverside Georgian villas on Grosvenor Road, with the latter two being listed structures. Further efforts must be taken to reduce the impact of any development on these residents."

They went on to criticise the lack of social housing. *"Given the housing pressures in Churchill Gardens, including serious overcrowding and long-standing residents being pushed into temporary housing, as well as a Westminster wide housing waiting list of over 4000, we believe that this scheme should provide new social housing (with a local lettings policy) to address this problem,"* they argued.

Finally, the Churchill Labour Councillors pointed out that, *"the only access for construction vehicles will be Churchill Gardens Road, which is a narrow road serves residents in Churchill Gardens estate and children going to St Gabriel's Primary School."*

In September, Liza continued her local campaigning with a call to the Council to help the local 'foodbank' Ebury Food Surplus. In a letter to the Council, Liza wrote,

"Many residents of Churchill Ward and in South Westminster rely on the Ebury Food Surplus. During lockdown, I, as well as many mutual aid volunteers, referred struggling families to Ebury Food Surplus. In recent weeks, Ebury Food Surplus has also been providing support for Afghan refugee families. The services Ebury Food Surplus provides to the community is vital and I am disappointed that they have not been offered a permanent space. I urge the Council to find a permanent space in South Westminster as soon as possible."

The following month, the proposed merger of two Catholic primary schools raised community concerns which were taken up by Robert Eagleton who had been selected as one of the three Labour Candidates for Pimlico South Ward, alongside Liza and Jason Williams (who had served as a Labour Councillor for Churchill Ward from 2014-2018). The proposed merger of the Westminster Cathedral and St Vincent De Paul Catholic primary schools was being considered because Westminster Cathedral School was under-subscribed and had a large financial deficit.

With government funding linked to student numbers, schools like Westminster Cathedral (and others in Westminster) faced pressure to merge and cut staffing levels. Robert Eagleton picked up the link between falling school rolls and the cost of housing, telling the local press, *"The parents I have spoken to are outraged at the proposals. Why is a 'Good' school, in a desirable part of central London, under-subscribed? The truth is, families are being forced out of Westminster because they cannot afford to live here. This is what happens when you re-house social tenants outside the borough and fail to build enough affordable housing".*

Jason Williams was delighted to be back on the campaign trail after his narrow defeat in 2018. In November he led a local campaign to stop raw sewage being pumped into the River Thames around Churchill Gardens, Dolphin Square and the Tachbrook Estate for over 1,000 hours. Highlighting the fact that, in 2020, sewage outlets around the Churchill Garden Estate, Dolphin Square, and the Tachbrook estate spilled raw sewage a shocking 242 times for over 1,050 hours cumulatively, Jason took local MP Nickie Aiken to task for failing to join the call to Government to stop the sewage dumping, saying, *"As a former Councillor and local resident, I have fought hard to tackle river pollution. Last year I launched a petition calling on the Council to clear up plastics near the riverbank. But it is hard to protect the environment when we have an MP who is unwilling to support vital votes in Parliament."*

In December, Jason took the opportunity to re-kindle an issue in which he had previously been involved, when Westminster Conservatives' flagship College, the £16 million Sir Simon Milton University Technical College (UTC) announced that it was to close three years after the Council had pushed the project through despite residents' concerns. The UTC closure meant that the Council's £2m expenditure on the school had been lost. Jason and other Labour Councillors had voiced concerns at the time, about the building itself, the financial shortfall in the project, and lack of social housing. Opened in 2017 and specialising in science, technology, engineering and maths, it was aimed at 14-to-19-year-olds. However, in the last academic year it had only 150 students on its roll, out of a capacity of 550.

The UTC was the brainchild of the Sir Simon Milton Foundation, a charity with close links to Westminster Conservatives. The charity's trustees include a roster of former councillors and officers. As Jason reminded the local press, *"We constantly raised residents' concerns about the UTC from the inadequate consultation process to the impact on local residents in Peabody Avenue, Abbots Manor and Westmoreland Triangle. At each stage our concerns were brushed aside while the Westminster Tories pushed ahead with this vanity project – even as other UTCs were having difficulties across London. We need an urgent plan for the site which includes local residents at every stage and for the council to genuinely listen and act."*

******

We ran campaigns in every ward. Our approach was, *'the next campaign starts the day after the election'*. So, Labour Councillors in Harrow Road, Church Street, Queen's Park, Maida Vale, Churchill, Bayswater, West End and Westbourne Wards had been running local campaigns for the previous four years, holding regular advice surgeries, attending residents' and tenants' association meetings, together with Ward Panels and ad hoc meetings to discuss highways and planning proposals. We developed a reputation for being available, for listening, for acting and for getting things done.

We kept in regular contact with residents through our monthly email *'Action Reports'* and we delivered newsletters with details of the issues we and Karen Buck MP were taking up. We were also available for residents in the Wards represented by Conservative Councillors, some of whom did not respond as sympathetically to their problems as we did. Throughout the campaign, I regularly took up issues on behalf of our candidates in the target wards, particularly in Lancaster Gate, Little Venice and Vincent Square Wards, feeding back responses from Council officers, Housing Associations and others to our candidates so they could respond to questions from residents.

One thing I learned very quickly was that responding speedily to constituents' enquiries was a sure way to impress. Our mantra was, *'Listen. Act. Communicate.'* As 'Tip' O'Neill's father said, *"All Politics is Local"*.

Chapter Six - Winning the West End

The West End has always been special to me. We used to come to London at Christmas when I was a teenager and stayed at the Regent Palace Hotel on Piccadilly Circus. My father had been stationed in London during the war, training as an RAF wireless operator, and he liked going back to visit old wartime haunts. We would drive down to London from Manchester on Christmas Eve after my parents had closed their newsagent's shop and arrive at around midnight. We would spend Christmas Day walking round the deserted famous West End streets, looking at the shop windows and eating at the Coventry Street Cornerhouse. On Boxing Day afternoon, we would drive back to Manchester. The West End 'bug' got me, too, and after I left school, I headed for the bright lights. I have been here ever since.

The West End Ward, comprising Soho, Mayfair and Fitzrovia, has always displayed a fiercely independent streak. In 1978, West End residents rebelled against what many felt was a complacent Council attitude to their concerns and elected two Independent Councillors, Gordon Viner and Lois Peltz. Gordon stood down in 1982 but Lois was re-elected in 1982 and 1986. The Conservatives did not take kindly to losing their West End 'province' and during the Shirley Porter days it sometimes felt that the Conservatives reserved their most poisonous venom for Lois and her supporters in the Mayfair Residents' Association.

The Conservatives won back the West End Ward in 1990 and had held it ever since, albeit with a few hiccups, including deselecting at least one rogue Councillor and another going to prison for benefit fraud. The Labour flag was always in evidence, but our electoral performance never threatened the Conservatives, despite the best efforts of local stalwarts David Bieda, Wendy Hardcastle, Dave Worton and Damian Dewhurst. Our main problem was that we always started our

West End election campaigns too late, giving our candidates no time to get known to residents or to develop a track record of achievement. This was particularly important in the narrow streets of Soho where tracking down voters on the upper floors above shops, cafes and restaurants needed time, patience and resilience in equal measure.

So, when in the summer of 2016, I heard from fellow Councillor Jason Williams that two new members, Pancho Lewis and Patrick Lilley, were interested in running to be Councillors in the West End, I jumped at the opportunity to encourage them. We arranged for the four of us to do a 'walkabout' in Soho and Fitzrovia where I pointed out the blocks of flats with social housing and talked about some of the local issues of which I was aware. I knew the Fitzrovia area especially well from my time as an unsuccessful candidate in the former Cavendish Ward in 1990 and 1994. We finished our walk at a restaurant on Great Titchfield Street and by the end of our meal Pancho and Patrick had decided to have a go. I could not have been more delighted.

Pancho and Patrick were a very unlikely pair. Pancho, in his late twenties, was a committed environmentalist with a strong academic and activist background in the UK and abroad. He had spent some time earning a living as a busker, playing the saxophone. Patrick, on the other hand, was in his fifties with a successful career as an events promoter and publicist. A strong gay rights activist, one of Patrick's 'claims to fame' was to have a shared a flat in Fitzrovia with Boy George, the Culture Club lead singer (before he was famous). Each had different skills and strengths and together they were definitely more than the sum of their parts.

Pancho and Patrick got to work straight away, knocking on doors and meeting residents. We put together a 'plan of action' of things to do which I knew would work – getting to know local 'opinion formers', writing letters to residents on local issues, organising petitions, briefing local journalists, delivering local newsletters. We identified issues that we would campaign on. Crucially, we decided to run three separate campaigns to reflect the diversity of the three distinct West End Ward communities of Soho, Mayfair and Fitzrovia. We also agreed to collect as many email addresses as possible so that we could keep in touch with residents through regular email *'Action Reports'*. With two years before the May 2018 Council elections, I was confident that we could make a real impact and run the Conservatives close.

The West End campaign soon got into gear with regular door knocking and newsletter delivery sessions arranged most weeks. Pancho, recruited many of his friends to the cause, so we regularly had half a dozen people out on the street, including his girlfriend Maggie Desmond (now his wife). Finding a third candidate was also a priority and Caroline Saville, who lived in Dolphin Square, was persuaded to join us. With a practical, common-sense approach, Caroline was the perfect foil to Pancho and Patrick's often 'runaway' enthusiasm.

In an interview in the 'Guardian' in July 2018, Pancho Lewis summed up his positive approach to the West End campaign. *"We refused to accept the assumption that the West End always has to be Conservative, and as soon as you [do that] you pave the way for things to be done differently,"* he said. *"Speak to people, engage with people, show them you are taking them seriously and can take action,"* he continued. *"Prove to people that things they thought weren't possible, are possible. It's a lot of hard work and it's often not particularly glamorous. But that's what it takes to win in places where people say you can't win."*

Patrick Butler's 'Guardian' article summarised the essentials of the 2016-2018 West End campaign, *"Success came on the back of two years of hard graft: he (Lewis) and his fellow Labour candidates became de facto councillors, meeting residents and immersing themselves in the unglamorous minutiae of ward business, from noise nuisance to street litter. His campaign arguably took off, however, after it tapped into* wider resident perceptions that the distinctive heritage of the area was being destroyed by unbridled commercialism. There was unhappiness that property developers were seemingly dictating local planning decisions, that corporate interests were encroaching on public space, and that Westminster council was in thrall to both."

The Labour campaign put the spotlight on the "hotelification" of the area – an ingenious slogan coined by Patrick Lilley. It shone a light on the new expensive 'corporate' hotels, the non-stop development of luxury flats which were often left empty by overseas investors, and the loss of well-known local shops, restaurants like the Gay Hussar, and other businesses through massive rent increases. In addition, the decline of the famous Berwick Street Market was a big local issue and the West End campaign gave its full support to Robin Smith's battle to save his 'Soho Dairy' stall in Berwick Street. In Mayfair, Pancho Lewis organised a petition to save the Curzon cinema which was under threat from its landlord. The petition received more than 27,000 signatures and was pivotal in persuading the landlords to back down – the Curzon was saved, at least for another few years.

The Labour campaign had a real impact. An often-heard complaint from traditional Conservative voters was they *"felt taken for granted and ignored by a remote and arrogant Council"*. Added to that was the turmoil inside the Conservative camp, when Conservative West End Councillor Paul Church claimed that he was *"bullied, silenced and threatened"* by colleagues when he tried to speak out against property developers. Another Conservative Councillor, Glenys Roberts, who had represented the West End Ward since 1999, also became a victim of the Conservative infighting and did not stand again in 2018. *"I resigned from the Council and the Tory party,"* she said. *"I tried to stand up for the residents against vested interests only to be marginalised and worse, but I was able to tell them some home truths that have come to haunt them, namely they would lose seats to Labour because everyone had had enough..."*

As a result of the internal chaos, the Conservatives did not select their three candidates until well into 2022 and when they did, Jonathan Glanz, the only surviving West End Conservative Councillor, announced on Twitter that he was pleased to take Tim Barnes and Hilary Su on a tour to 'familiarise them' with the West End – which drew a loud 'guffaw' from locals like Andrew Murray.

Election day itself was incredibly exciting. There was a real buzz, right from the beginning of the day. The team ran three campaign centres, and dozens of people came to help – some even from abroad. Pancho Lewis' brother, Emiliano, who had been helping with the campaign for many months, led the charge in the campaign centres, helping build real energy and momentum. There was a real sense that Labour might be able to make some gains.

The 2018 West End Ward result was so close. Tim Barnes topped the poll with 990 votes, with Pancho six votes behind with 984 votes and Jonathan Glanz taking the third seat with 973 votes. Patrick Lilley, with 947, missed out by 26 votes while Caroline received 927 votes. With an 18% swing, Labour's three candidates outvoted the Conservatives' three candidates by 2,858 to 2,801. The one independent candidate, campaigning against Oxford Street pedestrianisation, received 291 and it is likely that he took more votes from the Conservatives than from Labour. On the other hand, the Green Party candidate probably took more votes from Labour than from the Conservatives.

For the next four years, Pancho Lewis made the most of his position as Labour's first West End Ward Councillors. Looking back at his experience, Pancho recalled, *"The Council has begun to wake up to the fact that its overly cosy relationship with property developers is intolerable and that Soho demands better. As a result, we've seen significant progress. New measures were introduced to allow for more democratic accountability in the way planning decisions are made."* He argued, *"We also successfully lobbied the Council to introduce measures to protect Soho's character: the Council's City Plan now embraces a Soho 'Special Policy Area' which helps protect independent business shop units and in principle guards against large hotel planning applications, among other things."*

Listing some of his successes, Pancho said, *"We forced the Council to U-turn on its decision to severely cut back on opening hours for Marshall Street Leisure Centre. We successfully lobbied to regulate busking. And, after a prolonged battle, we got the Council to go back to the drawing board when it was feared that the 'al fresco' scheme was going to be made permanent without consultation."* Perhaps the biggest change Pancho was available to achieve was giving West End residents the belief that things could be different. *"For years, Soho and the wider West End was effectively a one-party state"* he said. *"Westminster Conservatives took Soho for granted, failing to curb the excesses of property development. Worse still, Council chiefs proactively promoted over-development, which severely eroded Soho's heritage and impacted community well-being. In recent years we have begun to turn the needle."*

In early 2021, Pancho and Patrick Lilley were reselected as candidates, alongside Jessica Toale, a Covent Garden resident. The selection meeting attracted 30 Labour members, a strong indicator of how the local community had been invigorated by the West End campaign – and how high the expectations now were.

Pancho, Patrick and Jessica were in 'campaign mode' from the outset. In March 2021, they organised a petition against the temporary 'al fresco' dining being made permanent. In July 2020, as a response to the pandemic which had done huge damage to West End hospitality businesses, Westminster Council introduced a street closure scheme to allow for al fresco dining. Labour supported this temporary move but urged the Council to listen to residents living in the streets affected. The Council promised that residents would be "at the heart" of their approach. Unfortunately, a combination of poor management of the scheme including the repeated violation of social distancing rules, inadequate access for disabled and elderly people, poor enforcement, extreme noise, and other issues, drove many residents to near breaking point during the temporary al fresco scheme.

The result can be best described as uncontrolled 'al fresco drinking' with many Soho streets packed with groups drinking into the early hours of the morning. Often, they brought their bottles of drink direct from local supermarkets. The Soho Society was very vocal on the problems caused, undertaking a survey which revealed that more than a third of resident respondents said that they would move out of Soho if the 'al fresco' scheme were to become permanent. Perhaps it's unsurprising then that among Soho residents the scheme became known as the Westminster Conservatives' 'al fiasco'.

Later that month, Pancho turned his attention to Mayfair where he launched a petition calling on the Council to take action to clamp down on the havoc caused by the Audley Square development where the Council was allowing repeated relaxation of the permitted hours of operation. This resulted in what residents experienced as an interminable extension of very noisy works, causing extreme disturbance and disruption. As the petition argued, *"The development has been going on for years. Enough is enough. Residents have had enough and demand that there is proper regulation of the development, not the free for all that is currently permitted – worse still, actively endorsed."*

The future of Oxford Street had been a constant issue since the Council abandoned the pedestrianisation plans immediately after the 2018 Council elections. In June 2021, the Council revealed a plan to create a new traffic-free 'Piazza' at Oxford Circus. There were concerns that the Council's plans for the Oxford Circus Piazza may well have improved the public realm in this iconic area, but there were real concerns that it may have also led to more taxis, delivery vans and other vehicles using the residential streets north and south of Oxford Street. Our belief was that creating the Oxford Street Piazza, stretching from John Prince's Street, next to the John Lewis store, for 150 metres all the way to Great Portland Street, vehicles would have to take a detour through the side streets to get to the other side of Oxford Circus. In our view, many drivers would decide to take alternative routes through the streets north and south Oxford Street to avoid the inevitable traffic jams.

Taxi drivers and white van delivery drivers would want to avoid the route around Oxford Circus and would soon find quicker routes through the residential streets of Marylebone, Fitzrovia, Mayfair and Soho. In addition, it was proposed that bus routes be re-routed in a circuitous way around the new Oxford Circus Piazza. This threatened to displace congestion and air pollution to neighbouring residential streets and cause delays to bus travellers. The Council's proposed use of a Temporary Traffic Order, which avoided the need for public consultation, was an added reason to oppose the Piazza proposals. Pancho told the local press, *"We have urged the City Council to fully consult with residents before starting on roadworks to implement these plans. We repeat our call to the Council to put community engagement at the forefront of plans for Oxford Street, including the Oxford Circus Piazza. Those who live and work in the area are the ones who will be most greatly affected by these plans and it is very important that they are properly consulted before changes are implemented that could have a significant impact on their lives."*

In the Summer of 2021, we had a real shock when Pancho announced that he would be standing down to study for a doctorate on environmental sustainability issues at Lancaster University, starting in the Autumn. We all knew that Pancho was absolutely committed to doing all he could to tackle the Climate Emergency. He had led the Labour Group thinking and action on Climate Emergency policy and was our most powerful advocate. But he was also at an important point in his life. He and his partner, Maggie, were planning to start a family. He knew that that would place new demands on his time, and, together with starting a doctorate, he felt it made sense to have more time to help with childcare if and when they did have children (as of July 2022 they have a baby daughter, Thomasin) Besides, if he did stick at it, run and win again in May 2022, did he see his future as a long-term Opposition Councillor, winning all the arguments but losing every vote?

Pancho was determined to see out his time as a West End Councillor, living in Soho, and combing his university studies with his Councillor duties. But now we had to find someone to fill Pancho's very big shoes. We were so lucky that waiting in the wings was Paul Fisher, a former Covent Garden resident who had been helping Judith, Shamsed and me in the Hyde Park 'decoy' campaign. Paul had shown his talents, experience and willingness to put in the work. Importantly, Patrick Lilley was impressed by Paul and provided advice on how to approach the West End ward membership in the selection process.

In August 2021, the 'rejigged' West End Team returned to the issue of 'al fresco' dining, now under the *Vision for Soho* banner, and urged the Council to maintain balance between needs of hospitality businesses and residents, following numerous complaints received by Pancho Lewis, particularly about noise levels. With a greater concentration of hospitality businesses than other parts of Westminster, The West End Labour Team argued that to build a sustainable future for the neighbourhood – where residents, hospitality businesses, and other businesses like post-production studios can co-exist harmoniously – it is necessary to balance the interests of every business sector and those who live in the area carefully and sensitively.

With that in mind, Paul, Patrick and Jessica wrote to the Council calling for the introduction of noise monitoring equipment on the streets worst affected by noise pollution. They asked for the data collected by noise monitoring equipment to form part of the Council's assessment about how to plan for Soho's future once the temporary road closures came to an end in September. In their letter, the West End Team wrote, *"On the streets most affected by road closures, including but not limited to Dean Street, Bateman Street, Frith Street, and Old Compton Street, extreme noise pollution is having a serious impact on residents' quality of life and in some cases their very mental health."* Acknowledging that living in Soho, residents must expect more noise than in the suburbs, the letter commented that, *"Residents in Soho have long accepted that their unique position at the heart of the city means being accommodating to the needs of hospitality businesses and that included a reasonable degree of activity, indeed more so than almost any other residents."*

The letter also made the strong point that, *"in some of the narrower streets the impact of the al fresco scheme has led to a dramatic change in their circumstances – that includes more people and crowds on the streets after streets reopen, a significant increase in people drinking and eating directly outside their homes on the street every day of the week, and more buskers and street entertainers often flouting rules around noise."*

Another Soho issue which the West End Team gave their support was the campaign to stop the demolition of 20th Century House in Soho Square. As Paul Fisher told the 'Soho Clarion', *"Campaigns to preserve buildings like 20th Century House are indeed about environmentalism, but they are also about preserving what makes Soho special: its history."* Jessica Toale agreed, *"The Council appears all too willing to allow heritage buildings to fall by the wayside in favour of commercial interests. And if the Council took its environmental commitments seriously, it wouldn't allow buildings like 20th Century House to face the threat of demolition when refurbishment would be a suitable alternative."*

In February 2022, another internal Council document found its way into the hands of Labour Councillors, this time revealing Council plans to close some Westminster Libraries, including in the West End. An internal paper entitled, *'Westminster Libraries and Archives: Overview of Transformation and Next Steps'*, outlined the key findings from the Council's review of the library service and made the case for major changes. It seemed that the Council had been quietly planning radical changes to Westminster's libraries – without any intention of telling people about them before Council elections on 5th May.

Based on the information in the document it was clear that the Council was preparing (a) to close Charing Cross Library and merge it with the Westminster Reference Library, (b) to close the Westminster Archives and removing the materials to an 'off-site' collection (c) to break their promise to replace the St James' Library and, importantly for West End voters, (d) to only extend the lease on Mayfair Library for a short-period with no commitment on its future.

This was big news for us. Libraries are a very special place for many people and Council plans to close Mayfair Library were bound to be a very effective campaigning tool. Pancho made the political point, *"Labour has promised to protect local services. By contrast, the Conservatives seem to want to close them down. The Council appears to have been quietly planning to close Mayfair library. We will safeguard its long-term viability and that of all libraries."* By only committing to a short-term extension of the lease for the Mayfair library, with no clarity about what might happen next, the Council made the mistake of leaving West End residents with uncertainty about its future. Patrick Lilley made another telling point, *"Mayfair Library is a huge community asset used by a multitude of local people and groups and should remain open. It's disturbing that its future is at risk."* Inevitably, we had a petition ready at hand.

Other campaigns supported by the West End Labour Team included the one to continue the Asset of Community Value status of the Soho Hospital for Women and the protection of independent shops and the revitalisation of Berwick Street Market as an essential amenity for residents and local businesses. As Patrick Lilley told the *'Soho Clarion'* in the Spring 2022 edition, *"I will encourage the large freeholders to give preference to independent retailers because that is what Soho is about."*

With the Council elections just weeks away, it was the Council's 'Vision for Soho' plans to reintroduce 'al fresco' dining across Soho that took centre stage, as it epitomised everything that was wrong with the Council's approach. As Pancho Lewis explained in his *'Soho Clarion'* article in Spring 2022,

"To restore trust the Council needs to stop and listen to people's concerns — not brush them aside as if they were mere inconveniences. But this is what they seem intent on doing. They are ploughing ahead with their so-called 'Vision for Soho' which would lead to huge changes to the area, despite deep scepticism about these plans from the community. This isn't the right way to proceed. Labour candidates have committed to introducing a moratorium on the 'Vision for Soho' plans if they're elected. In its place they'd lead proper and meaningful community conversations and work out how to proceed from there — not impose top-down, divisive plans."

With polling day fast approaching, in mid-April, former West End Conservative Councillor, Glenys Roberts dropped her 'bombshell' by publicly backing the Labour Candidates. *"For the past four years West End residents have been emailing me for help having had little satisfaction from their elected Tory councillors,"* she told voters. *"I have been very happy to work with Pancho Lewis who has taken a genuine interest in their quality of life. Jessica Toale, Paul Fisher and Patrick Lilley – who came within 27 votes of getting a second Labour seat last time — will be excellent successors. The West End deserves nothing but the best."*

Underlining the importance of the forthcoming Council election, Pancho Lewis reminded residents, *"The most significant threat to Soho is, however, not one single issue. It's bigger than that. The biggest risk is a return to the politics of the past — a return to Conservative one-party politics. If this happened, little could be done to prevent the Council from reverting to their old ways of taking the community for granted."* In deciding how to cast their vote, Pancho asked voters to answer a simple question, *"Do I want a return to the politics of previous decades, where the interests of big business were consistently put before the needs of the community, with very little if any real means of holding the Council to account? Or do I want representatives who will stand up and fight for Soho?"*

Chapter Seven – Taking on Hyde Park Conservatives

Taking on the Conservatives in Hyde Park Ward was very much a 'leap in the dark'. Apart from the Star Street area, where over the years I had picked occasional bits of casework, much of the rest of the ward was an unknown quantity. Of course, I had often walked through the Hyde Park Estate on our way to Hyde Park, passing through Connaught Square and the police on duty outside the Blairs' house. I had read about the problems with Airbnb in Park West and I had watched the new office and residential buildings go up in Paddington Basin. But I was very much on the outside, looking in.

I obviously knew the Ward Councillors, Heather Action, Ian Adams and Antonia Cox and got on with them all pretty well. I knew Ian the best through his past roles as a Cabinet Member, Scrutiny Committee Chair and Lord Mayor and always found him open to ideas, easy to discuss things with and unfailingly polite. There was an unconfirmed rumour that Ian had decided not to put his name forward for the 2022 Council elections.

I knew Heather and Antonia less well. Heather was always polite and friendly and appeared to me to be not a very 'political' Councillor. An experienced operator on the Council, she was considered to be a 'safe pair of hands' as Cabinet Member for Public Protection and Licensing. Previously Chair of the Marylebone Association, Heather had trod a familiar Westminster Conservative route from residents' association to Conservative Councillor and then on to the Cabinet.

Antonia, on the other hand, was a lot more political. A former Conservative Parliamentary Candidate in Islington, she was elected at a Council by-election in 2012 and looked to be set for a rapid move up the Council hierarchy. Very much a political activist, she was heavily involved in the 'Free School' movement which eventually saw the establishment of Marylebone Boys School in North Wharf Road of which she was a governor. In 2019, she was on the shortlist for selection to be the Conservative Parliamentary Candidate for the Cities of London and Westminster which Nickie Aiken won. There was no doubt, that we were taking on experienced and committed opponents.

We had very little information on the Conservatives' political activities in Hyde Park Ward, other than seeing occasional email newsletters which tended to be a rehash of Council announcements with very little specific news on local issues. We certainly got the impression that the Conservatives regarded Hyde Park Ward as a 'safe' Ward, where they could 'coast' from election to election doing the minimum. The 'minimum' seemed to consist of sending out irregular newsletters, responding to issues raised by their supporters, attending social events and keeping very much within their 'comfort zone'.

I am sure Heather, Ian and Antonia would dispute this and point to scores of local issues that they had taken up over the years. However, looking from the outside, we thought there was an opening to do things better and to contact those who felt forgotten on issues that had been ignored. We also believed that, although 'incumbency' can give sitting Councillors some advantages, it can also make you a defender of the Council and the status quo so that you miss or are blind to opportunities to fight on the side of residents.

****

During the Covid 'lockdown' in 2020, the quiet and generally tranquil Hyde Park Ward was hit by a major community 'fall out'. Proposals for a Low Traffic Neighbourhood (LTN) were announced by the Council which then proceeded to divide the community down the middle. Following extensive public consultation, Conservative Cabinet Member Councillor Andrew Smith took the decision to 'bin' the LTN scheme, telling residents, *"There have been many comments from across the community and, while there is a recognition that the volume of traffic passing through the area is an issue, it is clear there is not a consensus in support of the proposed scheme. We acknowledge the concerns that have been raised, and we have made the decision not to progress with the proposed Low Traffic Neighbourhood."*

On the one hand, the long-standing Hyde Park Estate Association (HPEA) welcomed the Council's decision not to proceed with the experimental LTN, arguing, *"the Council's proposed scheme did not solve the problem for significant numbers of people on our Estate, and threatened to cause traffic mayhem on the peripheral roads around our Estate, with predicted increases in pollution and detrimental knock-on effects for neighbouring communities."*

Explaining that there should be no losers in any future scheme, the HPEA said, *"All of the needs of our community must be served, and we cannot support any scheme that severely disadvantages any one group of residents over another group."* The HPEA recalled, *"We have for years been trying to get the Council to pay attention to our needs and acknowledge that the installation of cycle lanes in the wrong places has had the effect of funnelling traffic into residential areas."*

Taking a contrary view were an equally passionate group of residents who were keen to see the roll out of the experimental LTN, stating, *"An LTN changes the pecking order from 'car as king' to 'cars as guests' - with people coming first."* The LTN supporters argued, *"The Hyde Park estate low traffic neighbourhood was given a robust design, removing the 80% of traffic that currently cuts through the estate (while allowing access by vehicle to every street), and creating a new green public space on Connaught Street."* They also claimed, *"the engagement work - a clearly communicated design online giving people 4 weeks to respond with their views - was described by one transport professional as "the best I have ever seen"."*

The LTN supporters also poured scorn on the Council's argument that there was not a consensus in support of the proposed scheme, *"This should not come as a surprise. What bold (traffic) scheme anywhere has met with 100% approval - or anything like consensus - especially at such an early stage?"* was the withering repost.

There is no doubt that severe damage was done to local community relations. The Hyde Park Estate Association suffered resignations from its committee and the supporters of the LTN set up a new residents' association, Hyde Park Estate Residents (HyPER). HyPER sent a letter signed by over 200 residents to the Council supporting the LTN, arguing, *"This is where we need strong leadership. And conviction. If the council is waiting for a consensus, there will be no LTN, or any positive change, to any street in Westminster. Councillors should press on with a trial and take people with them, explaining their reasoning at every step, listening to residents and reasonably adjusting the scheme in response to concerns."*

Acknowledging the obvious rift in the community, which *"has created excitement and expectations for some, while creating dread and sheer rage for others",* the HPEA urged residents to put the events of the recent past behind them. *"Sadly, as a result, we have become a divided community. This, surely, is not how we should be. As neighbours in a small community, we need to work together for the common good, and exercise care and understanding for one another",* was the HPEA Chairman's plea.

All this had happened before 'Operation Hyde Park' was even a remote thought in our minds. As a result, we did not have to 'take sides' or disappoint anyone by taking the 'wrong side'. But the LTN issue had certainly created a sense of dissatisfaction among some residents and was certainly a factor in the May 2022 election campaign, creating the right context for a message about the 'time for change'.

****

While our Labour campaign got going in the late Spring of 2021, the hoped-for response from the Conservatives did not come until October when they announced their three Candidates. As expected, Ian Adams had decided not to stand for re-election, so Heather Acton and Antonia Cox were joined by new candidate Zaheed Nizar, a Westminster businessman This was followed by a new 'team photo' on their Facebook page, with the news that the Conservative Team was *"raising local concerns with our London Assembly member Tony Devenish".*

However, it was on 10th December 2021 that we were able to raise a huge cheer when news came in that the Conservatives had swallowed 'Operation Hyde Park', hook, line and sinker. We read the Hyde Park Conservatives' post on Facebook with real joy, *"Yesterday evening was 'SUPER THURSDAY CAMPAIGNING' in Hyde Park! A massive thank you to Leader of the Council, Councillor Rachael Robathan, and also fellow candidates and councillors from across South Westminster - Elizabeth Hitchcock, Murad Gassanly, Tom Davies, James Spencer & Greg Conary."* Our plan was working. We had forced the Conservatives to defend their 'safe' Hyde Park Ward, sending at least four experienced Councillors, including the Leader of the Council, to deliver leaflets and knock on doors. I posted the good news on our Labour Councillors' 'Slack' message board.

Further Conservative 'Super Thursday Campaigning' sessions followed regularly over the next few months attracting more experienced Conservative Councillors and campaigners to Hyde Park Ward. On 23rd December 2021, Conservative Councillors Elizabeth Hitchcock, Selina Short, Tony Devenish, Robert Rigby and Ian Adams took part in *"the last campaigning session in Hyde Park for 2021!"* A huge, huge thank you to our fellow Councillors from across North/South Westminster who joined us," the Facebook message proclaimed. A month later, on 20th January 2022, Council Leader Rachael Robathan, took her Knightsbridge & Belgravia ward colleagues to Hyde Park for another 'Super Thursday Campaigning', with *"fellow candidates and councillors from across South Westminster - Elizabeth Hitchcock, Louise Hyams, Tony Devenish, David Harvey, Ian Adams and Martin Hayes."* A few weeks' later, on 3rd February 2022, the 'Super Thursday Campaigning' in Hyde Park again comprised *"the Leader of the Council, Councillor Rachael Robathan, and also fellow candidates and councillors from across Westminster - Barbara Arzymanow, Tony Devenish, Ian Adams and Iain Bott."*

The regular presence of the three Knightsbridge & Belgravia Ward Councillors, Rachael Robathan, Tony Devenish and Elizabeth Hitchcock, in Hyde Park at the 'Super Thursday Campaigning' gave us great heart. The Conservatives were doing exactly what we wanted – campaigning in Hyde Park and not in the West End or any of the other of our target Wards. We believed that such a regular presence of experienced campaigners would surely boost the Conservative cause by enabling them to talk to voters, identify their supporters, sign up postal voters and reassure the doubters. Our efforts would probably win Labour extra votes, we thought, but the Conservatives' increased efforts would bear electoral fruits to them – or so we expected.

On 17th February, the Conservatives' continued their 'Super Thursday' canvassing in West End Quay. *"A big thank you to Councillors Elizabeth Hitchcock & Tim Mitchell for joining us. So good to hear from local people about what their local council can do for them,"* was the Facebook message. A month later, on 12th March, the Conservative Team was strengthened by the presence of Cities of London & Westminster Member of Parliament, Nickie Aiken, 'Knocking and Dropping' in Connaught Village. *"Amazing to have Councillor Ian Adams join us. And a massive thank you to the*

Leader of the Council, Cllr Rachael Robathan and our very own MP for Westminster, Nickie Aiken, for giving up their Saturday mornings and giving us a helping hand. We know how super busy all three are serving the City of Westminster," was the gushing praise for the outside help pouring into the Hyde Park Conservative campaign.

The Conservatives were certainly upping their activity. On 15th March 2022, their Facebook post announced, *"NEW FRONTIERS. Campaigning in the newly ward inherited Chapel, Transept & Cabbell Streets. GENUINELY listening to our newly acquired residents' concerns and delivering the message that a Conservative Council in 2022 will continue to deliver Safer Streets, Cleaner Streets, a Greener City, a Stronger Economy and the Lowest Council Tax in the UK."* And later that week, on 20th March, the Conservatives were *"Out and about this afternoon in Connaught Village and the surrounds for some Hyde Park Ward Campaigning! A massive thank you to the Leader of the Council, Councillor Rachael Robathan and Councillors Elizabeth Hitchcock and Barbara Arzymanow, for giving up their Sunday afternoon and giving us a helping hand."*

The Conservatives' Facebook posts were invariably photographs of themselves and their supporters, but rarely, if ever, identified the issues on which they were campaigning. On the other hand, our Facebook (and Twitter) posts featured the issues we were taking up, with occasional pictures of us out and about on the campaign trail. The only time the Conservative campaign mentioned an issue they were campaigning on was on 31st March 2022, when Councillors Rachael Robathan and Heather Acton and Zaheed Nizar were pictured at Downing Street. Zaheed Nizar explained, *"Only yesterday I was out in Park West on Edgware Road and this seems to be a very big problem for the residents in Park West. The short-term letting issue affects neighbours, essentially, it's not productive for any residents that live in our ward. We would like to see a register in place as soon as possible, and hopefully, this petition will go some way towards rectifying that."*

As the election got closer, we detected a more frantic and desperate Conservative message, occasionally bordering on the patronising. On 7th April, Facebook reported *"Heather Acton, Antonia Cox and Zaheed Nizar were out and about in Hyde Park today with our ward mascot. We were also joined by Councillor Tony Devenish! The message being delivered was a simple one: You have 3 votes on May 5th. Please vote wisely by voting for Heather Acton, Antonia Cox and Zaheed Nizar,"* Two days later, on 9th April, the Facebook post announced, *"SATURDAY MORNINGS in Hyde Park Ward with Heather Acton, Antonia Cox and Zaheed Nizar. Much better than watching SATURDAY MORNING TV! We get the opportunity to tell you about everything we have accomplished and also how we will continue to work hard for you."* The following day, 10th April, the Conservatives were, *"Back campaigning in Hyde Park Ward today! Thank you to Councillors Elizabeth Hitchcock & Barbara Arzymanow, and Dianne who joined us this afternoon. We continued to deliver the message that only a Conservative Council in Westminster will be able to continue to deliver the essential services our residents need."*

The Conservative 'heavy hitters' continued to make the Hyde Park campaign their priority. On 19th April, The Conservatives were 'Knocking & Dropping' in Hyde Park today with Leader of the Council, Councillor Rachael Robathan. *"Councillors Heather Acton & Antonia Cox already work extremely hard for residents in Hyde Park ward. And alongside Candidate Zaheed Nizar, they will continue to work hard for their residents. So let's keep Westminster Blue on May 5th, by casting your vote for Heather Acton, Antonia Cox and Zaheed Nizar."* Nickie Aiken MP made a further visit to Hyde Park on 23rd April and was joined by Rob Butler, Conservative Member of Parliament for Aylesbury. *"YOU HAVE THREE VOTES ON MAY 5th, so please use them wisely and vote Heather, Antonia & Zaheed"*, urged the Facebook post.

The final weeks of the campaign were predictably very frantic. By now, the Conservatives believed they were, unexpectedly, fighting for their political lives. Their Facebook message was simple and direct, *"So please keep Westminster Blue on May 5th, by casting your vote for Heather Acton, Antonia Cox and Zaheed Nizar. Only a Conservative Local Council will continue to deliver: A Greener City, A Growing Economy, A City with Cleaner Streets, A Safer City, A City that Cares for Everyone. And all for the lowest Council Tax in the UK. Your Council Your Choice"*

With six days to go, Facebook reported a self-serving message, *"Continuing THE FINAL PUSH in Hyde Park today, letting residents know that this election is about how well a Westminster Conservative Council can serve them LOCALLY in 2022. This election is ALL ABOUT LOCAL ISSUES THAT AFFECT OUR RESIDENTS ON THEIR DOORSTEPS. Let's keep Westminster Blue by putting your 'X' in the box".* The day before the election, on 4th May, the Conservatives' Facebook message became more desperate, *"All that we ask is that you vote for the party that can serve you best locally. Just look at our record and keep Westminster Conservative. Vote Heather, Antonia & Zaheed."*

It looked like the Conservatives had given little thought to their message. I would have understood if they had simply stuck to 'Vote Conservative for the lowest Council Tax in the UK', but the Facebook message from the Hyde Pak Conservative campaign was all about them, not about the voters. *"IN THIS FINAL WEEK, WE REMIND OUR WARD RESIDENTS THAT... Councillors Heather Acton & Antonia Cox already work extremely hard for residents in Hyde Park Ward. And alongside Candidate Zaheed Nizar, they will continue to work hard for their residents."* In addition, the message was all about the Conservative Party, *"So let's keep Westminster Blue on May 5".*

The Conservatives were pleading for loyalty from their supporter base. Their offer was simply 'more of the same' at a time when there was a general and genuine belief that it was 'time for change', locally and nationally.

Chapter Eight – "It's One Rule For Them……"

There is absolutely no doubt that the 'Partygate' scandal played a significant role in 'turning Westminster red' in May 2022. It was no surprise to us that Labour and Lib Dem-inclined voters were quick to tell us that they would be voting Labour to "get rid of Johnson", but it was what the regular Conservative voters said that took us aback. We did not knock on many doors in the more expensive parts of the Ward as we thought it would be a fruitless task. But when we did, we were surprised, even shocked, by the language used by some life-long Conservative voters.

I have done more than my fair share of canvassing in difficult terrain. Over the years, I have very rarely had the door slammed in my face. More usually, the response in solid Conservative areas was the polite confirmation that the resident would not be voting for the Labour candidate. But during March, April and May 2022, the responses from many Conservative voters were couched in a series of four-letter words prefacing the name 'Boris Johnson'. Most of the voters expressing their disgust with the Prime Minister's behaviour had a personal story of how they could not visit an elderly relative or attend the funeral of a family member because they "obeyed the rules". Very few of them were planning to vote Labour. They were simply refusing to vote. I lost count of how many times I heard, *"it's one rule for them, and another for the rest of us"*.

As one Pimlico South resident told the 'Standard' on 3rd May, *"I'm angry about Partygate and how they have been getting away with it when we got into so much trouble when we went out,"* he says, adding that two of his friends were fined and that the issue might convince him to go to the polling station on Thursday. *"Maybe my vote will make a difference.""*

The facts and figures of 'Partygate' are well known. While lockdowns were in place across the country, numerous gatherings took place in 10 Downing Street, in the garden at Downing Street and in nearby government buildings. *"Invites to "bring your own booze" to the Downing Street garden, suitcases wheeled in full of alcohol, "wine-time Fridays", a child's swing broken, "raucous karaoke" with Whitehall's head of propriety and ethics, and a senior aide DJ-ing in the basement at the leaving do for a spokesperson who now works for the Sun."* reported Jessica Elgot in the *'Guardian'*. Unbelievably, it was the Prime Minister's then principal private secretary who organised the 'Bring Your Own Booze' summer party.

In late January 2022, twelve gatherings were investigated by the Metropolitan Police, including at least three attended by Prime Minister Boris Johnson. As a result of the investigations, the police issued 126 fixed penalty notices to 83 individuals for offences under COVID-19 regulations. It is believed that some officials received up to five fines. Boris Johnson, his wife Carrie, and Rishi Sunak, the Chancellor of the Exchequer, were all issued with Fixed Penalty Notices. They apologised and paid the penalties.

Not only did the scale of the law-breaking by our leaders shock so many people, but it was the manner in which they thought they could get away with it that really cut through in the minds of the public. There was a string of denials that anything wrong had taken place. The stock response from the Prime Minister was that *"all rules had been followed"*, with a firm denial that any parties took place. Unfortunately for Johnson, a video of a mock press conference in 10 Downing Street surfaced soon after, featuring jokes about a party indeed having taken place. As Jessica Elgot commented, *"It is hard to fathom how the culture developed in the very offices where rules were drafted which banned families holding hands at funerals, saw women give birth alone and kept children apart from their dying parents."*

This was followed by a string of resignations. First to go was Allegra Stratton, Johnson's Downing Street Press Secretary, who appeared in the 'mock' press conference video. Next, Shaun Bailey resigned as Chair of the London Assembly's Police and Crime Committee after it was revealed that he had attended a gathering of Conservative Party staff. This was followed by the resignation of five senior Downing Street staff and the Parliamentary Under-Secretary of State for Justice.

Worse was to come when it was revealed that there were two 'party' events in Downing Street on 16 April 2021, the day before Prince Philip's funeral, during the third lockdown across England. The Prime Minister was forced to apologise to The Queen.

Then there was the 'Sue Gray report' conducted by senior civil servant Sue Gray. Gray's final report in May 2022 described multiple Downing Street and Whitehall events, including excessive drinking and a lack of respect shown to lowly cleaning and security staff. Sue Gray concluded that the nation's political and civil service leadership *"must bear responsibility for this culture"*.

At every opportunity, we 'rebranded' Westminster Conservatives as 'Boris Johnson's Westminster Conservatives', to underline the message that a vote in May for Westminster Conservative candidates was a vote of confidence in Boris Johnson.

We were very keen to turn up the volume on the 'Partygate' background noise locally as much as we could. At the Council meeting in January 2022, Labour Leader Adam Hug prized out of Council Leader Rachael Robathan her strong backing for Boris Johnson over the 'Partygate' scandal. Adam reminded Councillor Robathan that the lockdown rule-breaking parties, while others struggled to survive, had been met with fury by residents. To which she insisted Boris Johnson had acted *"quite rightly"* in his response to the scandal and praised him for setting up an inquiry into his presence at the parties.

****

While the Prime Minister tried to claw back his popularity with a forthright defence of Ukraine in the face of the Putin invasion, Councillor David Boothroyd dug out information on nearly £120,000 of donations accepted by Westminster Conservatives from Putin-linked sources. This was another opportunity to go on the offensive against the Westminster Conservatives.

On 23rd February 2022, the day before the Russian invasion of Ukraine, we called on Westminster Conservatives to give the Putin-linked donations to charity. Using information from the *'Daily Mail'*, the *'Guardian'* and Reuters, we identified four Putin-linked sources which had given the two Westminster Conservative Associations £118,491 over recent years. The Cities of London & Westminster Conservative Association (CLWCA) had received £76,764 since 2007, while Westminster North Conservative Association (WNCA) had received £41,727 since 2009.

The four Putin-linked donors were, first, Lubov Chernukhin, a former banker married to Putin's former Finance Minister. Her donations totalled £18,504. According to the *'Guardian'*, *"Chernukhin, reportedly donates enough to the Tories to qualify for membership of a small group of ultra-rich donors who meet monthly with Johnson and his chancellor, Rishi Sunak"*. Second, there was Lev Mikheev, an investment banker with links to the Kremlin who donated a total of £32,500. The *'Daily Mail'* reported that, *"Much of his fortune came through a hedge fund called Salute Capital Management, named after the former Soviet Union's space exploration programme Salyut, and he is reputed to have invested £1 billion a year on behalf of the new wave of wealthy clients to emerge under Putin's rule."*

George Piskov was the third donor to Westminster Conservatives. A banker who launched a money-transfer service across Russia and who donated a total of £7,377. *"He* formed a bank called Uniastrum, which became one of the fastest-growing businesses in Russia during these boom years, but ran into trouble during the global financial crash of 2007/08," according to the 'Daily Mail'. The fourth donor was Alexander Temerko, who had forged a career at the top of the Russian arms industry and had connections at the highest levels of the Kremlin. His donations, including those of one of his companies, totalled £60,110. According to Reuters, "Three former Russian business partners, said Temerko grew close with the Russian security services. Those ties were forged in the 1990s, these people said, when Temerko served as head of a state committee for the military and later as head of a strategic Russian state arms company known as Russkoye Oruzhie, or Russian Weapons."

Councillor David Boothroyd, Labour's Finance spokesperson, spoke for many when he told the local press, "I think people in Westminster might be shocked to know that Putin-linked businesses have funded the Conservative Party running their Council to the tune of nearly £120,000 in recent years. We call on Westminster Conservatives to return this money – not to the donors, but to charities supporting people in Ukraine."

The Conservatives remained silent on the Putin-linked donations, so we suggested to residents that they ask Conservative canvassers if Putin-linked money had paid for the election leaflets that were delivered through their door.

****

Closer to home, we continued to put the spotlight on the Conservatives' financial incompetence, a key element in our aim to neutralise the impact of the low Council Tax. In November 2021, figures presented to a Scrutiny Committee revealed that the Council had spent over £20 million on Oxford Street, with most of it going on expensive consultants. The figures presented to the Business and Children's Policy and Scrutiny Committee on 29th November 2021, reported to Councillors that the Council had spent £20.2 million on Oxford

Street with over £18 million going on consultants' fees. The Scrutiny Report revealed that £16.1 million was spent on Oxford Street *"feasibility design and staffing costs"* and a further £2.5 million was spent *"to develop Place Strategy & Concept Design"*. To add insult to injury, the Scrutiny Report informed the Committee that the £20.2 million *"does not include the £6 million allocation for Marble Arch Mound which will be funded from the overall Oxford Street District allocation"*.

The Scrutiny report admitted that the only 'outcomes' from the £20.2 million Oxford Street expenditure are *"Construction of Oxford Street footway widening, planting and seating, Soho Photography Quarter and Berners Street/Newman Street traffic switch"*. Sitting on the Committee as a substitute for a colleague who was unable to attend, I was outraged by the huge amount of money that had been spent with so little achieved. I told the press, *"Over £20 million has been spent on Oxford Street and there is very little to show for it other than temporary pavement widening and a few planters and seats. Over £18 million has gone on expensive consultants to draw up plans and 'strategies'. Boris Johnson's Westminster Conservatives cannot be allowed in charge of public money for a moment longer. The May 2022 Council elections cannot come too soon."*

Another by-product of the Council's obsession with Marble Arch was the subsequent failure of the Council to make a successful bid to Government for 'Levelling Up' funds. In January 2022, the Council heard that its bid for £20 million focussed on the Marble Arch end of Oxford Street had been turned down by the Government. The Government's 'Levelling Up Fund' was devised to help deprived areas, and eight out of Westminster's 20 wards have neighbourhoods among the most deprived in Britain. But Westminster Conservatives' bid ignored these vital facts. It was no wonder that the Council's bid targeting the Marble Arch end of Oxford Street and focussed on improving the 'visitor experience' was turned down flat by the Government.

Councillor David Boothroyd made the point, *"Westminster Conservatives have lost sight of the priorities of the residents they should be serving. Invited to put forward projects that would help improve the lives of people suffering deprivation, they put forward their extravagant, but vague plans for Oxford Street. The Government's fund is more suited to supporting local high streets in the hearts of our local communities such as Harrow Road, Queensway, Westbourne Grove, Lupus Street and Edgware Road. Clearly the Government agrees that no-one wastes money quite like Westminster's Conservative councillors."* And to make the point even stronger, David added: *"This pathetic failure finally disproves the Conservative Party's line to voters that you need a Conservative-run Council to get on with a Conservative government."*

At times, it felt as if the Conservatives were handing us opportunities on a weekly basis. In October 2021, we called on the Council to pull the plug on plans to redevelop Huguenot House, near Leicester Square, into a £100m casino complex. The scheme, to redevelop Huguenot House's flats, cinema and shops, would cost £100 million to demolish the building and replace it with a high-rise mega-casino complex. Labour Group Leader Councillor Adam Hug wrote to the Council's Chief Executive and Director of Finance to argue, *"it is our strong view that a casino would not be an appropriate use of Westminster Council-owned land. A casino would not only add to anti-social behaviour in the immediate area around Huguenot House, it would also set an extremely bad example for the Council to be providing further venues for gambling in this way."* Adam also reinforced the 'financial competence' argument. *"Given the Council's embarrassing failure to deliver value for money with the £6 million Marble Arch Mound,"* he said, *"there is no reason to trust Westminster Conservatives with this £100m high risk gamble with tax-payers' money. This out-of-touch scheme is yet further proof that Westminster Conservatives have been in power for far too long and that it is time for a change."*

We felt in control of the message, our campaigning was going well in our 'target' wards, the Conservatives were in disarray nationally and we had successfully lured local Conservatives to defend their 'safe' Hyde Park Ward that we did not expect to win. We were on our way to a very good result. But no one dared utter, or even whisper, the words 'Win' or 'Victory'. The mountain was, in our minds, still too steep to climb.

Chapter Nine – The Home Straight

At the end of March 2022, the local election campaign entered the 'home straight', or the 'short campaign' as it is known in technical terms. During the 'short campaign' every penny of expenditure is required to be accounted for to keep within the strict election expenditure limits set out in law. We were fortunate in having experienced election agents, Andy Whitely, Margaret Lynch, Jaqueline Bore and Connor Jones to plan our 'short campaign' expenditure and to guide candidates through the myriad of forms to sign. In addition, beavering away in our Shirland Mews headquarters, our election organiser, Dario Goodwin (who was also a candidate in Lancaster Gate Ward), prepared canvass sheets, organised the design and printing of election leaflets and managed our growing social media output.

Our Manifesto writing was led by Labour Group Leader Adam Hug who coordinated contributions and wrote much of the document himself. A key element of the Manifesto was the Climate Emergency section on which Ryan Jude and Pancho Lewis led the thinking and drafting, with important contributions from Cara Sanquest and Max Sullivan. It was important for us to do more than offer 'warm words' about tackling this fundamental issue. We wanted to put forward a 'blueprint' for action that would be taken by a Labour Council. In particular, we wanted to persuade potential Green Party voters and Liberal Democrats that voting Labour would be a positive act and that this was a priority for us.

Our Communications Group met online weekly at 6pm every Monday evening for half an hour to discuss the week's programme of press releases, social media posts, events and activities. We developed a 'grid' of policy announcements and media statements so that our key messages were repeated at the critical times. Again, it was Campaign Organiser Dario Goodwin who played a vital role in translating our Communications ideas and plans into action.

We launched our Election Manifesto, *'Labour's Plan for a Fairer Westminster',* on Saturday 12th March at the University of Westminster in Regent Street, where Shadow Foreign Secretary David Lammy MP, Westminster North MP Karen Buck and Westminster Labour Group Leader Councillor Adam Hug, set out Labour's plans for the 2022 Council elections. Our key pledges were:

- Freezing Westminster's Council Tax until 2024 to help with the cost-of-living crisis.
- Building more Council and key worker homes to give families a future in Westminster.
- Putting the needs of residents before developers in the planning system.
- Keeping our area safe with more police to tackle knife crime and Council action on anti-social behaviour and rubbish dumping
- Standing up for better NHS services against cuts and sell-offs.
- Reinvigorating our neighbourhood high streets to better serve local people, with more jobs and more green spaces to spend time in.
- Protecting private renters through more action against bad landlords and rogue letting agents.
- Improving opportunities for children and young people and support our older and vulnerable people.
- Placing the climate emergency at the centre of the Council's work by mandating low carbon developments, urgently retrofitting homes and cleaning our air.

With the £6 Million Marble Arch Mound still visible as its long-awaited demolition progressed, we reminded residents, *"Every four years, residents have the chance to sack those running the Council. There has never been a more obvious time for*

Westminster residents to exercise their power. When things go wrong, those making the decisions should carry the can. On 5th May, Westminster residents will have 6 million reasons to sack Boris Johnson's Conservatives."

Our campaign teams were redoubling their efforts on a regular basis as we sought to win the target Wards. We had a great team, including many young, able and enthusiastic candidates. It certainly felt like our best campaign since 1986 when we came within 106 votes of becoming the largest party. Canvassers and leaflet deliverers were out daily, with morning and afternoon 'shifts' at the weekends. There were visits from Labour Front Benchers, Anneliese Dodds MP and Johnny Reynolds MP. The Westminster area was buzzing with excitement. At the same time, expectations were rising. The *'Standard'* dusted off an article that appeared regularly every four years. *"Ahead of the 2022 local elections, Conservative peer and political analyst Lord Robert Hayward suggested that Westminster was one of four Conservative strongholds in London that was at risk of being won by Labour in the wake of the 'partygate' scandal,"* the *'Standard'* proclaimed.

We had seen this all before, particularly in 1990 when the Conservatives were able to claim spectacular victories in Westminster and Wandsworth to cover up a disasterous set of Council election results nationally in the wake of the Poll Tax. We knew the Conservative Central Office 'playbook' off by heart. They would say that Westminster was 'in play' and then claim a great victory when the votes had been counted and the Conservatives were re-elected to rule Westminster for another four years.

We wanted to play down all talk of Labour winning Westminster. Fortunately, the 'Standard' article included a very sensible 'health warning', arguing, *"Despite the optimism surrounding Labour in Westminster ahead of May 5, an uneven distribution of core support in the borough could hamper the party's chances of making substantial gains. With* the majority of Labour's support located in the northwest of the borough, very few seats appear to actually be marginal."

I was very keen to underline the 'health warning' with whomever I spoke, not least because I genuinely believed we would not win, despite 'Partygate', despite the Mound and despite the positive noises we were hearing on the doorstep. I met *'On London'* editor Dave Hill in Bayswater in mid-April and his subsequent article helpfully led with, *"Could the Conservatives lose control of Westminster Council? It's easier to describe how they might be defeated – something that's never happened before – than it is to believe it will happen. Local and national factors look helpful to Keir Starmer's party, but some pretty distant stars will have to align if it is to win next Thursday."*

It was helpful, too, to read Dave Hill report, *"informed judges – such as Philip Cowley, Lewis Baston and Ben Walker of Britain Elects – anticipate Labour falling short in Westminster and why Dimoldenberg has a good case for dampening expectations."*

At our meeting, I set out the electoral arithmetic which Dave summarised succinctly, *"There are 18 three-seat wards being contested in 2022, which means Labour would need to win 28 out of the 54 seats to secure a historic majority. They can depend on retaining 15 of those they already have: all three in the Queen's Park, Church Street, Westbourne and Harrow Road wards and the slightly less certain Maida Vale. Then come the varyingly marginal wards where the battle with the Tories is most intense."*

"In two of these," Dave Hill explained, *"Labour gained one of the three seats in 2018 and will need to take the lot this time: Bayswater and the symbolically potent West End. That would bring their total up to 21 seats, which would be their biggest haul since 1986, the year Labour has come nearest to seizing the Tory fortress at the heart of the UK capital."*

Hill continued, *"Also on the Labour target list is Lancaster Gate ward, adjoining Bayswater, which returned a trio of Tories four years ago. Labour will have to emulate that to get to 24 seats. A further hat trick will be required in the newly-created ward of Pimlico South, assembled from the now abolished Churchill ward, where Labour won 2-1 in 2018, and part of the similarly expunged Tachbrook, where the Tories won 3-0."*

Concluding his electoral analysis, Dave Hill wrote, *"If Labour hit all of those 12 target seats, the result would be a 27-all draw and an interesting constitutional situation. To secure a majority next Thursday Labour would also have to wring a single seat out of a strongly Tory ward to bring their total up to a majority-clinching 28. They have chosen as their best bets Vincent Square, Little Venice and Hyde Park."*

In my comments to Dave Hill, I told him candidly, *"We've got a mountain to climb. We need all the stars to be aligned to pull it off. I'm pretty confident we'll run them close in the popular vote, but we could still end up with just a third of the seats."* As Dave Hill explained, *"Projections based on successive huge London-wide opinion poll leads for Labour, fail to take into account the uneven distribution of support for the two big parties across the Westminster wards. In 2018, for example, Labour received 41.1% of the popular vote compared to the Tories' 42.8% but won only 19 seats while the Tories won 41 and retained a fat majority."*

Dave Hill signed off his article with some helpful information about what was going on in the Conservative camp. *"Westminster is, very simply, a Tory bedrock and it would be a true political earthquake if it turned red next week. Could the earthquake actually happen? Although the answer is probably no, the Tories have good reason for some concern. The Marble Arch Mound debacle has done them no favours and a Lancaster Gate Tory activist has reportedly confided fears that, in his own words, "a lot of our people are away" – a reference to second home-owners heading for the country during the pandemic, not coming back and maybe not sorting out a postal vote. "*

The fact that many Conservative voters had remained in their second homes in the country was not something we had picked up. Most of my door-knocking had been on Council and Housing Association flats, where our priority was to ensure that those who were eligible to do so registered to vote and applied for a postal vote. Coming across doors where no one every responded was not new to us, given the large number of second homes and pied-a-teres owned by foreign nationals and people who worked in London during the week and returned home at weekends. However, the phenomenon of long-time Westminster residents leaving for their second homes during the pandemic and not returning was totally new. If they had not arranged a postal vote themselves, it would have been very difficult for the Conservatives to contact them to encourage them to do so.

It may seem obvious, but 'Getting out the Vote' is key to winning elections. Or, as Lyndon Johnson once said, *"the first rule of politics is to be able to count"*. Traditionally, the Conservatives had been much better than Labour in getting residents to sign up for postal votes. But we were getting better. Voter turnout in Council elections is much lower than in General Elections, with many voters not bothering or not seeing what goes on at their local Council as important. Our colleagues in Hammersmith & Fulham attributed their 2014 and 2018 Council victories to encouraging Labour supporters to register for an 'early vote' – essentially, giving people more time to cast their vote. The 'rule of thumb' is that voters are twice as likely to vote if they have a postal vote. That is a very powerful reason to spend time urging your supporters to register for a postal vote. In his selection speech in the West End Ward, Patrick Lilley told this story,

"Most people are not interested in politics like us. Its Saturday afternoon and we are in a political meeting, so yes, we are different. So, the challenge is both emotional and practical to

speak to the other 99%. We have about 2,000 people in West End ward who voted Labour in 2019. I spent many nights out there on the streets, campaigning in the rain, to get a Labour government. But we failed. I won't let us fail in the West End. Two thirds of our supporters don't actually vote in Westminster Council elections - to be honest, they are not that bothered.

But once a person has a postal vote, they are more than twice as likely to vote in a local election. If we get 200 people to register for postal votes, we will get an extra 75 votes. That is enough to beat the Conservatives. It's that simple, but takes time, one person at a time. Last night I spoke to Miriam from Mayfair who is 85. She can't attend today as she is digitally excluded. But we sent her and 99 other members, a postal vote application form, which she used. Miriam can vote early and safely. Postal votes beat Trump. It was things like that that helped Pancho and I get an 18% swing to Labour in 2018."

****

The West End Ward campaign continued to pick up pace, with Andrew Murray reporting in his *'State of Soho'* blog, *"in recent years there has been genuine competition in a ward which Conservatives used to take for granted. Candidates and their supporters have been pounding the streets, if not in desperation at least at an indication that there is all to play for. There has even been a running (and sometimes amusing) spat on Twitter involving ex-Conservative councillor Glenys Roberts, whose endorsement of Labour candidates has not gone down well with some."*

Summarising the key issues, Murray reported, unsurprisingly, that the 'Partygate' issue loomed large. *"The Prime Minister's conduct over the so-called Partygate incidents has further revealed a style of leadership that is highly questionable. This is less about whether he has actually broken the law (which is obviously significant) but more to do with the culture surrounding Boris Johnson, in Downing Street and in his party more widely, and his attitude and behaviour in response to the Partygate publicity,"* commented Murray.

"Any decent primary school teacher could have established and made public the basic facts in an afternoon," he argued. *"If he had wanted to, Mr Johnson could have done just that. But instead of openness and honesty there has been characteristic bluster and evasion which has brought the office of Prime Minister into disrepute. Much of what he and his defenders have said has brought widespread public derision and, worse, increased the hurt and anger felt by many at the original revelations. And his party has retained him in office."*

The depth of the hole that Johnson had dug for the Conservatives was revealed at the hustings meeting. Murray reported, *"Until last week, as far as I am aware (and I'm happy to be corrected), there had been no public recognition by anyone in the local party that Boris Johnson was unfit to hold the position. That changed at the hustings held in Soho last week. To their credit, all three West End Conservative candidates finally said that if they were Boris Johnson they would resign. If not exactly a call for his resignation, it's a clear indication, in public, that he is unfit for his office."*

The key local issues were also very predictable. It was good to see that the Mound had, in Andrew Murray's view, made *"the Conservatives clearly more vulnerable on finance now."* He also expressed his *"surprise that the Conservatives defended it so vigorously without a great deal of credibility, and that the councillor responsible is standing for re-election."* Murray was also critical of the *"£3 million to upgrade a small area around the Photographers Gallery ……. while other streets in the area in much more need of repair have waited for years. Are there more effective ways to spend this sort of money?"* Murray also criticised the Conservatives' claim that the Council Tax could rise to the level of neighbouring boroughs under Labour. *"There is a map towards the end of their manifesto which gives that misleading impression,"* he argued. *"It's an* unworthy scare tactic, which has been used before and is the sort of thing that breeds distrust in politics."

The other major West End Ward issue was housing, with Andrew Murray pointing out that *"Council housing is not mentioned by the Conservatives, but they do intend to make 'Housing Associations improve their services to tenants in Westminster'."* This 'pledge' drew a stinging barb from Murray, *"Frankly, this is a bit of a cheek,"* he said. *"Housing associations may need to improve, but you would have thought that the first priority of the council was to improve their own housing service."* As a Council tenant in Kemp House, Berwick Street, Murray could cite, *"Personal experience in recent months is that only about 25% of issues I've been involved with in my block could be said to have been dealt with efficiently."*

Another key issue was refuse collection, with Murray arguing, *"'Maintaining our City's clean streets': this part of the Conservative campaign just doesn't work in Soho. Litter is dealt with reasonably well by our street sweepers, but there's no solution yet to the problems created by rubbish bags on the street awaiting collection. And especially near some hospitality venues our pavements are filthy. That's not to mention street urination, and the rest."*

On the long-standing pedicab nuisance, Murray gave *"full credit to MP Nickie Aiken for pushing for legislation to regulate pedicabs, though announcing 'victory' is a bit premature, as there is still some way to go before it becomes law."* On Mayfair Library, Murray was *"uneasy about the way Labour has pushed this issue. It was reasonable to raise concerns about possible closure, but it feels like these have been stretched in an unreasonable and 'political' way, given the robust and confident response that the library will not close."*

Finally, on the 'Vision for Soho' and the future of 'al fresco' dining and pedestrianisation, Andrew Murray made the key point. *"What is obvious about this,"* he said. *"Is that there is significant lack of confidence in the process. Soho residents are not a group with one single view on possible changes but, historically, not taking proper account of the local knowledge we have has proved a great mistake on more than one occasion."* Continuing on this theme, Murray pointed to the *"most direct references to the West End in the party manifestos. For the Conservatives: 'We will work with businesses of all sizes to support the recovery of the West End'. Labour's aim: 'Revive the West End and protect it from over commercialisation to keep it special'."*

Signing off, Andrew admitted, *"I still haven't finally made up my mind how to vote, which won't come as a surprise to people who know me well. When there are genuine choices to be made, I do like to mull over all the issues and the options and tend to be last minute in coming to a conclusion."* I tend to think that Andrew was an exception, with the vast majority of voters having already decided which way to vote.

****

In the Hyde Park Ward, Judith, Shamsed and I continued canvassing residents in our 'heartlands' of Star Street and St Michael's Street and in the new Housing Association property in Sheldon Square, North Wharf Road, Hermitage Street, Harbet Street and Paddington Gardens. Most of the social housing was occupied by families and, most importantly, they were all living here in Westminster, not in a distant second home. We were joined on the campaign trail by Judith's daughter and her adult children and we were getting a warm welcome wherever we went. The offer of postal votes went down very well, with some people very happy 'to vote from home'.

We were also getting a warm reception from former Labour voters who had abandoned us during the Corbyn years and who saw Keir Starmer as a person they could trust. The change in Labour Party leadership also attracted the 'floating voters' who decided their vote from election to election depending on the issues of the day. Labour was no longer a 'toxic brand' in the eyes of mainstream voters. During the entire campaign, I can recall getting an angry rebuff from just two voters in St George's Fields, bemoaning the fact that Corbyn "had been brought down by a media conspiracy."

We also decided to set up roving 'street stalls' outside Waitrose on Edgware Road and outside Le Pain Quotidien on Connaught Street. We met people from all over London standing on the Edgware Road, so that had limited local election benefits (although we registered a lot of Labour support from across London and south-east from people working and visiting London!). The Connaught Street location was much better in starting conversations with local residents, including people in the 'posher' parts of the Ward, who we had not canvassed but who were keen to tell us they were voting Labour this time. We handed out our local leaflets with our six pledges:

- Freeze Council Tax for all residents until 2024
- No more financial waste like the £6 million Marble Arch Mound
- Stop illegal rubbish dumping with heavy fines
- Safer streets with more police to tackle crime
- Deliver cleaner air and greener transport
- Put the needs of residents ahead of developers

We also continued taking up local issues and building up our email list. In the final months of the campaign our monthly email 'Action Reports' became bi-monthly as the scale of our casework increased. And the response from residents continued to encourage us,

"Great work as always. Fingers crossed — you HAVE to get elected. Lots of love from Bathurst Mews"

"I am constantly impressed by the amount of local actions that you initiate and follow through, for the good of us all. Thank you."

"Good luck with the upcoming election."

"We are back by the end of April in time to vote for you!"

"We posted our postal votes today. We both voted for the three of you, so fingers crossed"

"You are doing such a demonstrably excellent job working for our communities and you are also holding the Tory Council to account. I do hope that the three of you get elected",

"Both my husband and I follow the Action Report of the Hyde Park Labour team. We know that you have been actively dealing with all sorts of problems. We greatly appreciate all the support that you and your team have been offering to us and the community"

"I have been asking for information for years. That's the most information I have had so thank you. Thanks for all your help."

"You have my vote for definite and I will ensure I attend the polling station to vote for Labour!"

"Amazing work guys. Will certainly be voting for you."

In the middle of April, Linda and I went on a long-delayed holiday to southern Spain which was originally booked for April 2020 but was cancelled twice because of the Covid lockdown. We had a great week-long holiday visiting Seville, Cordoba and Granada. I even had time for long-distance campaigning, responding to emails and posting on Facebook.

In the last week of the campaign, we wrote to our 600 email contacts to share some of the key issues we had picked after speaking to thousands of residents since we launched our campaign. Locally, our campaign of 'getting things done' for Hyde Park Ward residents certainly struck a chord. Residents on the Hyde Park Estate, in the Star Street area and around Paddington Basin all told us that they appreciated the quick, efficient and positive service they have been getting from their Labour candidates. Our email said:

"Whether it is getting rubbish picked up, fixing broken streetlights or helping to get overdue housing repairs done, residents deserve a first-class service – and this is what we have aimed to provide. As one resident told us: "You are the only ones in all my years of living here that have ever acted on something that I have requested. Thank you. As a result, I am on this occasion changing my vote. All three of you will have my support. Action like you took deserves recognition."

Picking up on 'Partygate', we reminded voters, *"On the national stage, there is no doubt that there is huge dissatisfaction with Boris Johnson from life-long Conservatives, many of whom will be voting Labour on 5th May or staying at home. We cannot print some of the language used by former Conservative voters about Johnson. So many people really do want to teach the Prime Minister a lesson. 'Floating voters' are coming our way after working out that Labour is best placed to beat the Conservatives in Hyde Park ward."*

We concluded by arguing, *"many residents do believe that it is time for change in Westminster. For many, the £6 million Marble Arch Mound disaster was the 'last straw'. How could so much money be wasted on a failed project when it could have been much better spent on more police on the streets and residents' other top priorities. The Conservatives have been in charge for so long they have become complacent, often taking residents for granted. If nothing else, the Labour campaign in Hyde Park has attacked that Conservative complacency and entitlement head on."* Our final words were, *"It has been a privilege to serve you for the past year as*

Labour Candidates. All we ask is the opportunity to serve you as your Councillors."

The Westminster Labour campaign ended with Councillor Adam Hug restating our pledges, in particular, *"to put the interests of residents first if we win on Thursday. If elected, we will freeze the Council tax until 2024 to help tackle the Conservative's cost of living crisis."* Adam also repeated the 'time for change' message coupled with the reminder that a vote for the Conservatives was a vote of confidence in Boris Johnson, *"many people are fed-up with Boris Johnson's Conservatives here in Westminster who have been wasting your money and taking you for fools. They have become tired, out-of-touch and incompetent, wasting £6m on the Marble Arch Mound while local people struggle with rising bills. It's time for change and only Labour can beat the Conservatives here in Westminster."*

So, on 4th May, we looked forward to the election, anticipating a good result, but not expecting to win. We knew we had put up a good fight. We knew we could do no more. It was now up to the voters (or at least those who had not already voted by post).

Chapter Ten – Election Day....and Night

It was a chilly morning when I made my way to the Polling Station at the Pentecostal Church on Harrow Road at 7am. This was a new location for voters to get to know but it was handily placed for many of the new flats in Paddington Basin, particularly for residents in Montgomery House and Dudley House, two social housing blocks on either side of the Church.

With everyone else working in the target Wards, there was just Judith, Shamsed, Judith's daughter and Linda and me in Hyde Park Ward, where we spent the day at the two polling stations and 'knocking up' Labour supporters.

Voting was slow in the first few hours and I didn't know what to make of it. Were our supporters reluctant to vote after all? Had our supporters voted by post already? Was it Conservative voters who were not voting? Or had they all voted by post already? So many questions for which there were no answers. Did it matter anyway? We were not going to win. My only concern was that the Hyde Park result might end up being a complete humiliation for us.

After a few hours on the polling station my wife Linda took over from me and I delivered 'Vote today' leaflets around the social housing blocks and then started knocking on doors in Montgomery House. Despite reminding people in the weeks before election day that the polling station was literally next door, it was necessary to repeat the simple request that it would "only take a few minutes to go downstairs to cast your vote". 'Knocking up' always works and it remains one of politics' simple pleasures when you see the people you have spoken to on their way back from the polling station and they say, *"I have just voted for you"*.

In the afternoon I went back to the polling station and chatted with one of the Conservative tellers, Knightsbridge & Belgravia Ward Councillor Elizabeth Hitchcock. Elizabeth had been a regular canvasser and leaflet deliverer in Hyde Park Ward, so she knew the true state of the Conservative campaign. We didn't talk at all about the likely result, but I think I made it clear that I did not expect to win and she didn't disagree. We spent most of the time talking about her job as a Parliamentary Assistant to Matt Hancock MP. Sadly, Elizabeth failed to reveal anything new about the beleaguered former Secretary of State for Health.

In the late afternoon, I went over to the other Hyde Park Ward polling station at St John's Church Hall, in Hyde Park Crescent. Very much at the heart of Conservative territory, the polling station was altogether much busier, with Conservative tellers appearing to know everyone by name, guiding their flock to the ballot boxes like sheepdogs. If it has been like this all day, we have surely lost – and badly, was my immediate thought. I did not stay long and decided that my efforts would be better deployed in one of our target Wards. So, at around 6pm, I decided to 'call it a day' in Hyde Park Ward. It had been a great campaign. I had given everything. But there was no point in doing anything further. The objective of forcing the Conservatives to defend one of their safest Wards had been achieved, right up to the close of the polls.

I spent the evening in West End Ward. Arriving at David Bieda's house in Dean Street, Soho, the local campaign headquarters, at around 7pm, I pounded the streets for the next few hours with Paul Spence, one of our St James's Ward candidates, calling on residents in Broadwick Street, Brewer Street and Berwick Street. We managed to persuade a few more Labour supporters to vote for Paul Fisher, Patrick Lilley and Jessica Toale, as we made our way through the Thursday night Soho crowds enjoying a few drinks after work.

At around 9pm I left Soho and caught a bus to Victoria Street to be at the Count at Lindley Hall in the Royal Agricultural Halls in Vincent Square for 10pm. Not having eaten much all day, I stopped off for a Big Mac and then prepared for a long night. Our instructions from election agent Andy Whitely were to be at the Count early so that we could be there for the opening of the ballot boxes and the start of the vote verification process. Lindley Hall was a hive of activity and noise with the vote counters chatting away as they lined up at the trestle tables waiting for the delivery of the ballot boxes.

I went up to the press gallery on the mezzanine floor to see if they had any thoughts on the turn-out and the result. The first person I saw was Jonathan Prynn of the *'Standard'* who I had known for many years. He asked me if I thought we had won and I gave him my honest opinion, *"I think we have done very well across Westminster, but we will just fall short"*. I said the same thing to Local Democracy Reporter Hannah Neary who had been covering Westminster politics for many months.

Going into the Count, I believed we had a very good chance of winning 24 seats – 15 in the current Labour Wards – Queen's Park, Harrow Road, Westbourne, Church Street and Maida Vale, together with all nine seats in the currently 'split' Bayswater, Pimlico South and West End Wards. From the amount of effort that had gone into Lancaster Gate Ward, I thought we might possibly win that Ward, too, bringing us up to 27 seats. But we would need one more seat from either Little Venice, Vincent Square and Hyde Park Wards to win a majority and, based on my election day experience in Hyde Park Ward, I thought that was very unlikely. So, my best guess at the result was probably 30 seats for the Conservatives to Labour's 24 seats, with an outside chance of 27 seats each for the Conservatives and Labour. This would give the current Conservative Lord Mayor the casting vote at the first Council meeting of the new Council thereby continuing the Conservatives' unbroken 64-year rule for another four years.

The Hyde Park Ward count was in the far corner of the vast complex and Judith, her husband Mohammed, Shamsed and I positioned ourselves opposite the vote counters. Alongside us were the three Conservative Councillors and a few of their young supporters. As the ballot boxes were emptied on to the tables, we prepared ourselves for the last instalment of our adventure. The first part of the count is the 'verification' when all the ballot papers are counted to check that the number of ballot papers issued to voters at the polling stations is the same number that came out of the ballot boxes.

The ballot papers were counted 'face up' so the Party representatives can see them. This gives the Party representatives a general indication of how their Party is doing. There were three ballot boxes to be opened – two from the two polling stations and one with postal votes. As the ballot papers were counted, the young Conservative representative sat next to me was noting down how the votes were splitting between the three Parties. Looking over his shoulder, I was very pleased to see that we had done well on the 679 postal votes that had been cast and the result would not be the humiliation I had feared. But I still felt that the Conservatives would win as they seemed to have the edge on us.

Once the 'verification' stage had been completed, the Returning Officer was able to work out the voter 'turn out', which in Hyde Park Ward, was 29.5%, down from 31.4% in 2018. The key question was, who were the 2% who had not voted at this election? Before we could answer that question, the election staff had brought out the blue, red and yellow boxes where each ballot paper would be placed if all three votes went to the three candidates from each party. 'Split votes', where voters have voted for, say, one Labour, one Conservative and one Liberal Democrat (or any other combination of parties), would be placed in a separate box and counted individually later.

At this point of the process, the key job of Party representatives is to watch the ballot papers going into your opponents' box. If you see a ballot paper which, say, had two crosses for the Conservative candidates and another cross next to the Labour candidate, your job is to point this out to the vote counters so it could be checked. I was sat next to

Heather Acton during this process and there were very few occasions when either of us had to ask the vote counters to review what they had done. What was evident to both of us, however, was that the result was going to be very close, with the Conservative and Labour piles of votes matching each other as the votes were counted.

Once all the votes had been placed in the coloured Party boxes, the counting started, with votes counted in bundles of 20. Then the bundles of 20 votes were put into bundles of 100. The bundles of 100 were then placed on top of each other. At the end of the vote counting, the Labour and Conservative piles each had 600 votes. But the Labour pile had three additional bundles of 20s on top. It was at this point, that I thought we had a real chance of victory. At the same time, I knew this was not the end of the story.

Throughout our campaign we were at pains to remind voters they had three votes and they should use them for their three Labour candidates. Many people were surprised to learn they had three votes. When people vote at General Elections they have just one vote and, for some, the 'one vote' habit is difficult to break. As a result, many of the Hyde Park Ward electors voted for just one candidate, usually for the person highest up the ballot paper for the Party they support. On the other hand, having three votes gives some people the opportunity to spread their votes across the Parties. For example, they might be Conservatives, but they appreciated the help they received from one of the Labour candidates and so they will give one of their votes to that Labour candidate.

Despite our constant reminders to our supporters, *"You have 3 votes. Use them all for Labour",* there were many 'split' votes to count and, depending on how the individual votes were spread, the Labour lead of 60 votes could be whittled away if the three Conservative candidates picked up more individual votes than us. With her name at the top of the ballot paper, I thought that it very possible that Heather Acton could overtake us all. Counting the 'split' votes was a long and detailed process. For each individual ballot paper, one vote counter called out the names of the candidates who had a cross by their name, while another vote counter, pencil in hand, recorded the votes on a spread sheet. All this was done in view of the Party representatives so the tally of individual votes could be seen by all of us. Heather Acton was catching us up, and Shamsed was receiving more individual votes than Judith and me. But it was looking very good for all three of us.

The Council officer in charge of the Hyde Park Ward count then proceeded to add the tally of individual votes to the bundles of votes by party that had been counted early to come to a final result. At the end of that process, which seemed to take forever, all three of us emerged ahead, Shamsed by 46 votes, me by 22 votes and Judith by just 16 votes ahead of Heather Acton, the highest placed Conservative candidate. There was no call from the Conservatives for a recount. The Conservative candidates accepted defeat gracefully, we shook hands and they then left the Count even before the result was declared.

Md Shamsed Chowdhury - Labour   804
Paul Dimoldenberg - Labour   780
Judith Southern - Labour   774
Heather Acton - Conservative   758
Antonia Cox - Conservative   709
Zaheed Nizar - Conservative   659
Lib Dem   249
Lib Dem   240
Lib Dem   165

To say we were in shock would be an understatement. This was not the plan. We had never spoken about the possibility of winning, even if we had privately dreamed of pulling off such a coup. The news soon started to percolate across the hall and our colleagues came over to congratulate us. It was not long before the *'Standard'* tweeted, *"Labour are now on the brink of a stunning win in Westminster after taking all three*

Hyde Park council seats, according to my colleague Jonathan Prynn."

Chapter Eleven – An Historic Victory

Although we knew at about 2.00am that we had won the Hyde Park Ward, the result was not formally announced until it was light, at around 6am in the morning. But throughout the early hours of Friday 6th May, a run of Labour successes was declared by the Returning Officer and we could sense things moving our way. The results in the Labour-held wards were some of our best ever. In Queen's Park, Church Street, Harrow Road and Westbourne Wards the Labour candidates won around 65-70% of the vote. In Maida Vale Ward, which had been Conservative from 1990 - 2014, Geoff and Nafsika won over 60% of the vote, with new candidate, Iman Less, winning 55% of the vote.

Great victories in Labour wards were all very well, but it was the results in the marginal and target wards which would decide whether we could secure an historic victory. Indeed, my 'nightmare scenario' was, having won Hyde Park Ward, we would fail to hold our marginal Wards or lose in the target Wards, condemning me to four more years in Opposition. It was a mixture of emotions; delight at having won, fear of being on the losing side again. This would have been the ultimate 'fail better' result.

The marginals were certainly going our way. The result in Bayswater Ward was an absolute triumph for the work Maggie Carman had put in as the lone Labour Councillor in the Ward for the previous four years. After unfavourable boundary changes, Maggie secured a magnificent 1,618 votes and, together with Max Sullivan and James Small-Edwards, who received 1,481 and 1,476 votes respectively, were elected for all three seats with well over 50% of the vote. The three Conservative candidates trailed behind badly with 910, 875 and 792 votes, with the three Liberal Democrats on 276, 266 and 219 votes.

In the West End Ward, where four years previously Patrick Lilley had lost by just 26 votes, the years of hard work had paid off and Patrick, Paul Fisher and Jessica Toale were elected with over 47% of the vote. Paul Fisher topped the poll with 1,158 votes, with Patrick and Jessica both each securing 1,111 votes. The three Conservative Candidates were significantly behind with 961, 923 and 911 votes each and the three Liberal Democrats trailed in third with 264, 207 and 158 votes each.

The result in Pimlico South was closer. Liza Begum topped the poll with a stunning 1,516 votes, followed by Robert Eagleton on 1,426 votes and third, former Councillor Jason Williams, who was defeated by 9 votes four years earlier, securing 1,350 votes. The highest Conservative candidate was 79 votes behind Jason with 1,271, with the other two candidates getting 1,268 and 1,252 votes each and the three Liberal Democrats limping home with 252, 216 and 207 votes.

Wins in the five Labour-held Wards, three wins in the marginals, plus Hyde Park Ward, gave us 27 seats, exactly half the seats on the Council. But we still needed one more seat for victory. The votes were still being counted in Lancaster Gate, Little Venice and Vincent Square Wards, and they were all too close to call.

The result in Lancaster Gate Ward went to a recount before it could be declared, with just a handful of votes between the Labour and Conservative candidates for the third place. When the result was declared, two Labour Candidates were elected, along with one Conservative who topped the poll with 1,110 votes. Ellie Ormsby was the second placed candidate with 1,057 votes and Ryan Jude was third with 1,053 votes. Just two votes behind Ryan was one of the Conservative candidates, with the third Conservative candidate trailing with 980 votes. Again, the Liberal Democrats' three candidates were in distant third place with 319, 182 and 159 votes. A complicating factor was the presence of a single Green Party candidate who secured 303 votes, usually at the expense of the third candidate from each party, including Labour's Dario Goodwin who won 1,031 votes and was not elected despite the hard work he put in as Labour's Campaign Organiser.

With victory secured, the results at Little Venice and Vincent Square Wards were no longer as significant as they might have been. But the election shocks and surprises were not over yet. I had always regarded both Little Venice and Vincent Square Wards as 'difficult nuts to crack'. Both had been long-time Conservative strongholds and, in both cases, our campaigns had started late with candidates not in place until the end of 2021. Even with energetic and focused candidates, less than six months is not sufficient time to mount an effective, winning campaign.

In Little Venice, however, Sara Hassan, to her total surprise, won one of the seats with 1,104 votes, not far behind the two Conservatives with 1,140 and 1,136 votes each. The third Conservative candidate was fourth with 1,088 votes, with Rosie Wrighting, 1,071 votes, and Murad Qureshi, 1,053 votes close behind. The Liberal Democrats did poorly, winning just 231, 196 and 161 votes each. After the result was declared, Sara, who had been ill on election night, said, *"I was 100% sure I'd lost, then I got a phone call from Murad, 'Congratulations Councillor Hassan'. He told me to get down there pronto."*

And In Vincent Square Ward, Gillian Arrindell secured second place with 1,324 votes between two Conservatives who received 1,377 and 1,305 votes each. The third Conservative candidate was fourth with 1,297 votes and David Parton (1,232 votes) and Ananthi Paskaralingham (1,155 votes) followed. The Liberal Democrats were at the bottom of the poll with 371, 271 and 269 votes each. I have no doubt that if we had started just a few months earlier in Little Venice and Vincent Square Wards we could have won all three seats in both Wards.

Overall, the facts and figures were beyond our wildest dreams,

- 12 Labour gains, giving us 31 Labour Councillors
- The Conservatives reduced to just 23 Councillors
- A Labour majority of 8 seats
- Labour secured 48% of the vote, compared to 40.3% for the Conservatives

There was little time to take in the enormity of the result. We left The Royal Agricultural Halls at around 8am and sat in the sun outside a café on Victoria Street to get much needed injections of coffee and croissants. New Council Leader Adam Hug told the press, *"It is an absolute honour to become Leader Elect of Westminster City Council and my thanks go to the people of this great city who have placed their faith in me and my colleagues. I will seek to repay their trust by ensuring the interests of all communities are at the heart of everything the council does so that we deliver a fairer Westminster. Engaging local people in decision making and seeking new ideas from everyone in the city will be central to our fresh approach. I can't wait to get started."*

Later that day I spoke to Tom Foot of the 'Westminster Extra' and told him,
"To turn Hyde Park red, it's just well… I was thinking of that famous Michael Caine line: 'You're only supposed to blow the bloody doors off!' Well, we blew more than the bloody doors off. We turned Westminster red."

Now the hard work was to start.

****

The response to our election victory was overwhelming. Along with Labour successes in Wandsworth and Barnet, the trio of Labour Council wins led the national and local news all day and into the weekend, too. The *'Standard's'* Jonathan Prynn summed up the enormity of what we had done, writing, *"Until today, Labour had never run the local authority that had become a true blue Tory fortress over the 58 years since the Council was formed in 1964."*

Very few people expected our victory. John Zamit, Chairman of the South East Bayswater Residents' Association told readers of the Summer Edition of 'SEBRA News', *"Very early on the morning of 6 May, I was awoken by a telephone call from a property developer to tell me that Labour had taken control of Westminster City Council. I assumed he was joking! Turning on the TV with bleary eyes, I saw that it was not a joke!"*

Tim Lord, Chair of the Soho Society, had a similar early morning shock, *"Waking up early on Friday 6 May many of us were surprised to learn that not only had voters in the West End Ward returned three Labour Councillors, but voters in Westminster as a whole had selected 31 Labour Councillors and 23 Conservative ones."*

There were phone calls, emails, texts and messages of congratulations from all over. From old friends and former Council colleagues all wanting to share the moment. There was even time for a few celebratory drinks.

Among the many very kind messages were a number from former Council staff who I had worked with over the years, including three former Chief Executives, one of whom wrote, *"I'd heard rumours of your retirement – impossible to imagine and now actually impossible!"*. Another former chief officer wrote, *"The smile on your face on the internet said it all"*. It was also nice to get a letter from former Conservative Council Leader Nickie Aiken MP saying, *"I can't completely believe that I'm writing this letter to you!! And I'm sure you can't quite believe it either!"*

On Saturday, we were in City Hall for the first Labour Group meeting and later that week, Council Leader Adam Hug announced the Labour Cabinet. Adam Hug had been a councillor for Westbourne Ward since 2010 and had been

Leader of the Labour Group since 2015, having previously served as Deputy Leader and Shadow Cabinet Member for Adult Social Care and Public Protection. All of Adam's appointments were experienced Councillors who had acted as Shadow spokespersons in Opposition, so were very familiar with their new responsibilities.

Adam appointed his two Deputies to key roles. Tim Roca, a councillor for Harrow Road Ward since 2015 was appointed Cabinet Member for Young People, Learning and Leisure. Before becoming the Council's Deputy Leader and Cabinet Member for Children's Services, Leisure and Culture, he was Shadow Cabinet Member for Children's Services.

Aicha Less, was appointed Deputy Leader and Cabinet Member for Communities and Public Protection. Councillor Aicha Less had represented Church Street Ward since 2016. Before her appointment as Deputy Leader and Cabinet Member for Communities and Public Protection, she was the Shadow Cabinet Member for Public Protection and Licensing, and Children and Young people.

Nafsika Butler-Thalassis was appointed Cabinet Member for Adult Social Care, Public Health and Voluntary Sector. Councillor Nafsika Butler-Thalassis was first elected as a councillor for Maida Vale Ward in 2018. Before her Cabinet Member appointment, she was the Shadow Cabinet Member for Family Services and Public Health.

Adam appointed Geoff Barraclough the Cabinet Member for Planning and Economic Development. Geoff was first elected as a councillor for Maida Vale Ward in 2018 and was previously the Labour spokesperson on planning and business.

David Boothroyd was appointed Cabinet Member for Finance and Council Reform. David had been a councillor for Westbourne Ward since 2002 and was Labour spokesperson on finance before becoming cabinet member.

Liza Begum was appointed Cabinet Member for Housing Services. Liza was first elected as a Churchill Ward councillor in 2021. Following the elections in May 2022, she now represented the new ward of Pimlico South. Prior to becoming the Cabinet Member for Housing Services, she was the Shadow Cabinet Member for Housing.

Matt Noble was appointed Chief Whip and Cabinet Member for Climate Action, Regeneration and Renters. He had represented the Church Street Ward since 2018 and was previously Shadow Cabinet Member for Regeneration and Property.

Finally, I was appointed Cabinet Member for City Management and Air Quality, the area I had 'shadowed' in Opposition. Adam also gave me and my Deputy, Max Sullivan, responsibility for overseeing the Council's communications. Max works in advertising and I work in public relations, so we knew the territory. So, after over 30 years as a Councillor, stretching back to the early 1980s, I was in the Cabinet! It took me a while to take this in. I had a permanent smile on my face for over a week.

Adam also appointed Deputy Cabinet Members, together with Lead Members. With some really great new Councillors swelling our ranks and giving us additional skills and experience, we were all ready to go.

Perhaps of all Adam's early decisions, the most outstanding was the one to put forward Queen's Park Councillor Hamza Taouzzale as Lord Mayor. Born and bred on the Lisson Green Estate and of Moroccan heritage, he would be both the first Muslim Lord Mayor and, at 22 years old, the youngest ever holder of the post. First elected in 2018, as an 18-year-old, he had recently completed his Masters in Global Affairs at King's College London. Elected as Youth Mayor in 2016, Hamza drew huge respect across the Council Chamber for his considered, thoughtful and sometimes provocative Council contributions. He might only have been 22 years old, but he had the wisdom and gravitas of someone twice his age.

Importantly, too, Hamza's election as Lord Mayor signalled a new approach from the new Labour Council. He said, *"I do want to get out far more in the community, to be more visible in areas where the Lord Mayor isn't normally seen. I want to open this up and get people from the community to join me at events. And as an ordinary working class local I especially want to show young people that there are opportunities out there for them and to make a difference."* And no one could argue with his hope that *"I'm hoping that I'll get out and meet lots of new people and have some fun too."* As Andrew Murray commented in his *'Soho Clarion'* election review, *"The times they are a-changin'!"*

At the first Council meeting after the election on 18th May, Hamza was duly elected Lord Mayor and I moved the motion that Adam Hug be elected Leader of the Council. The Council Chamber at the London Business School on Marylebone Road was full of friends and relatives, including many former Labour Councillors from the past. I started by congratulating my former Queen's Park colleague, Hamza, on his election as Lord Mayor. I then made the off-the-cuff comment, *"What a great retirement this is turning out to be"*, which even got a smile out of the glum Conservatives.

In my speech, I acknowledged the many Labour Councillors who had preceded us. *"Our victory was built on the shoulders of the Labour giants who have come before us and who never gave up in the efforts to build Labour in Westminster and give proper representation to the 'many',"* I said. *"It is a great tragedy that Joe Hegarty, a Church Street Councillor for 16 years and Labour Leader from 1981-1987, died last year and cannot join our celebrations. Joe led the Labour Group which came within 106 votes of becoming the largest party in 1986. Joe was best Labour Leader in my years as a Councillor,"* I told the Council.

I also acknowledged the *"outpouring of goodwill towards the new Labour Council."* *"A Labour Council with a new purpose to change Westminster for the better has captured the imagination of staff across the board,"* I declared. *"We have even heard of two members of staff who have withdrawn their retirement requests so they can continue to work for the new Council. It is truly humbling."* The Chief Executive later told me that he doubted the veracity of this statement. However, at the time it was one of those stories that was 'too good to check'.

But I saved the best to the last. I had been waiting to say this for decades.

"Imagine Socialists running Buckingham Palace, militants lording over Parliament and controlling Downing Streets, left-wing extremists interfering with the daily running of business; a horrible nightmare. It certainly is but it could happen to the City of Westminster." So wrote Shirley Porter in March 1988 as she took her begging bowl round local business to raise money for her 1990 Council election campaign.

Talking about the 27 Labour Councillors, Porter said: "They are expert at manipulating the press and presenting an apparently respectable face to gain public sympathy. They cannot be underestimated".

Thirty-four years later, and here we are in Labour Westminster. With Boris Johnson, the first occupant of Downing Street to be a constituent of a Labour Council. Shirley Porter's prediction has finally come true. But I do have to disappoint you. We have no intention of running Buckingham Palace (although I was there last Wednesday at the Garden Party) or of controlling Downing Street (well, not until Keir Starmer is elected Prime Minister) or interfering with business."

As I sat down, I concluded, *"As we embark on this journey, one that we have worked so hard for, I close with the words of the late John Smith, 'The opportunity to serve – that is all we ask'. We now have that opportunity and we will strive hard over the next four years to make life better for Westminster residents in so many ways."*

My motion that Adam Hug be elected Leader of the City Council was agreed. In his first speech as Leader of the Council, Adam pledged policies to embrace all Westminster residents and alleviate poverty and housing need. The new Council's priorities would tackle the housing crisis, poverty and cost of living issues, the revival of retail areas across the area, and an *"urgent review"* of plans for redesigning Oxford Street inherited from the Conservatives. Adam promised to govern for *"the whole of Westminster"* and to put *"the priorities of our residents first"*. He also looked to take action in support of the deprived areas of Westminster, *"for too long many parts of our city have been overlooked by those in power"* and committed to *"tackling the massive inequality that has existed for too long in Westminster"*. He also confirmed that Council Tax would be frozen in 2023-24.

Adam identified housing problems as being *"particularly acute in Westminster"* and reminded the Council of decades of the Conservatives' failure to invest in *"the social housing that it desperately needs to tackle overcrowding and homelessness"*. He also promised action to *"support private renters who are facing spiralling rents and too often are not being treated fairly"*. He also said Labour wanted to *"give new opportunities for families to build a life in our city"*.

****

Our stall was set out and our intentions were clear, but first some thoughts on the reasons for our victory.

In his 'Soho Clarion' election review, Andrew Murray was clear that it was the Conservatives' actions that had lost the election for them. *"In power for too long, the Conservative leadership kept making mistakes and finally ran out of road. Resident groups across the borough had highlighted a lack of serious* engagement, as the council prioritised business over communities; the £6 million Mound fiasco undermined claims to financial competence; and, in campaigning, the focus on 'clean streets' was an own goal, for example," concluded Murray.

National issues played an important role, too, according to Andrew. "And then there was Boris. It was all too easy to connect the attitude of the Prime Minister with the party of Shirley Porter and Robert Davis, and some voters heard the silence from today's Conservative group and decided they wanted a different culture at City Hall," was Murray's analysis.

And speaking of Labour's West End success, he took the view that, "after making progress in 2018, Labour realised that if they put the effort in they could get still more reward and seriously upped their game again."

In their election review, the winning Lancaster Gate Labour Councillors, Ryan Jude and Ellie Ormsby identified some key factors. First, was our 'All Politics is Local' maxim'. "At the heart of a smoothly organised campaign we had a keen focus on local issues, enthusiastic candidates and activists and an ambitious vision for a fairer borough." Second was the decision to select candidates early, "Westminster was the first council in London to select its candidates – in spring/summer 2021. This allowed us to embed ourselves within the ward, build a personal presence and to help people with casework their Conservative councillors had been neglecting. By the short campaign, we could point to ways we had helped individuals in every area of our ward."

The third reason for Labour's success, according to Jude and Ormsby, was the inclusive and diverse approach to candidate selection, "Labour offered the most diverse slate of candidates in memory, with the resulting elected Labour members being 50% women, over 30% from ethnic minority backgrounds, and all age groups represented. A group that truly represents Westminster's diverse community." Fourth, came the Labour manifesto which promised, *"A council that properly consults and engages with residents on decisions, that embeds climate action in everything it does, builds truly affordable housing for the community, provides opportunities for young people and keeps the area safe. All while freezing council tax to help with the rising cost of living, and spending residents' money more efficiently."*

Finally, Jude and Ormsby agreed with Andrew Murray's conclusion that Boris Johnson was largely responsible for the Conservatives' defeat. *"The national picture and personal unpopularity of Boris Johnson was a theme that emerged throughout our year-long campaign. Numerous long-standing Conservative voters expressed at best apathy and at worst disgust with the current leadership. This, along with our local Conservatives' disastrous and wasteful £6m Marble Arch Mound project, approved amidst many other cuts, played a factor locally. We even saw some Conservatives switch to Labour for the first ever time,"* was their verdict.

In my 'Labour List' article in June, I identified many of the same reasons for our victory. Our concentration on local issues certainly hit home with the voters. *"We quickly realised that we were making an impression when residents started to tell us that "at last, someone is listening to us", "thanks for taking an interest in our concerns" and "thanks for replying to our emails, the other lot never do". Some of the issues residents brought to us were very small, but if you can get the small things fixed, it shows you can get things done. And 'we get things done' soon became our campaign slogan,"* was my firm conclusion.

We got a deserved reputation for action. *"No issue was too small. Every organisation that needed to improve its service, public or private, was in our sights. Invariably, our requests for action to sort out a problem were acted upon. And that boosted our claim that 'we get things done'! By election day, we had taken up hundreds of individual cases, which galvanised and enthused Labour supporters and turned Tories, Lib Dems and Greens into Labour voters."*

Second, regular communications with residents were a vital part of our campaign. *"We delivered six editions of our bi-monthly newsletter, 'Hyde Park Matters', to every house and flat in the ward. We posted daily Facebook and Twitter stories updating residents on the local issues we were taking up. We wrote to our local newspaper, 'Westminster Extra', every week about the issues that were of top concern to residents. Our letters were printed every week. We sent monthly 'action reports' to our email database. We started the campaign with less than 100 email addresses, but our list grew to nearly 600 by election day."*

And the third reason for our success was good organisation. We were very fortunate to have the help and advice of Margaret Lynch, a former Labour organiser, as our agent. At every canvassing session, we encouraged our supporters to apply for a postal vote. Voter turnout on the day was just 30%, but postal voter turnout was 60%. So, Labour supporters were twice as likely to vote if they had a postal vote. Our majorities were slim, so the effectiveness of the postal vote campaign cannot be underestimated.

Finally, I identified three other reasons that contributed to our success. First, like Ryan Jude and Ellie Ormsby, I agreed that *"starting early is so important. Early candidate selections are vital to give yourself time to understand the issues, develop contacts and make your mark. Rushing around for a frantic few months impresses few people. Starting early enables you to say: "We don't just come round at election time.""*

Second, *'little and often' was our campaign mantra – and this enabled us to pace ourselves and incorporate our politics with our daily lives. Our campaign was based on an hour here and an hour there, regularly over the 14-month campaign."* And third, *"nothing beats face-to-face contact. Knocking on doors and talking to voters provides you with the raw material on which to build your campaign. Listen to what people say, take action, and then tell them what you have done."*

In a post-election interview with the *'New Statesman'*, Adam Hug stressed the importance of our targeted approach to widen the Labour base. *"We have had to grow our electoral coalition,"* he explained. *"If we [had done] a base turnout campaign, we could have spent all our time knocking here on the Brunel estate and boosted the turnout. We could have won the popular vote easily by piling up the votes in our safe wards, but we still would have lost the election with fewer seats."*

Walking through the streets of Bayswater, on the border of Notting Hill, Adam Hug explained how our campaign also benefitted from a change in national politics. *"Some of these people will have voted for Blair at his height, moved to Cameron, then come on the return journey back because of Brexit,"* he argued, *"There's a shift in the Conservative Party at the moment, where it seems to be trying its hardest to annoy people who previously would've voted for it – the affluent urbanites who might live in smart mews houses, the "professional families who are anti-Brexit, socially liberal and believe in probity in public office."*

Writing in the 'Guardian', the weekend after the election, Matthew Weaver spoke to voters in Maida Vale Ward and found a mix of local and national factors to explain Labour's success.

"I was very happy when I woke up and found out Labour had won," says Nahid Poladi. She was appalled by the council's decision to spend £6m on a mound at Marble Arch. *"It was horrendous and really bad taste. I love art. I think live art is lifesaving, but that was monstrous. And anyone could see that it was tasteless."*

"Kamel Abdelaoui, the owner of a hardware store, voted Labour because of the cost of living crisis. "I've been

disappointed with the Conservatives [over] the cost of living," he says. "They have let a lot of people down. People are really struggling with money and they spent all that on a mound, it was ridiculous. We are tired of the Conservative party and how they have been lying in parliament. I hope Labour will do good things here now."

"Jacqui Gough says: "I just hope it sends a message that the Conservatives shouldn't be in government. Locally, the Conservatives have been quite good, they've cleaned up the canal and the rates have been very reasonable. I was thinking this morning that I bet they will go up, but we can afford to pay. And we should spend more on services."

Annikka Kauppinen agrees. "I had never voted Labour before," she says. "But I have really changed my mind in the last few years. We should be paying teachers and doctors and nurses. I don't mind paying more council tax if they spend it on services. I just think we need investment. If people lose patience, you see the rise of the far right, and that really scares me. And Boris is a buffoon."

Winning Council seats in Bayswater, Lancaster Gate, West End and Hyde Park Wards are strong evidence that our campaign attracted a wide spectrum of support from across the political divide, stretching from "Remain-voting urban liberals" to "the more socially conservative and Leave-voting working class." Winning again in 2026 would depend whether we could keep that coalition together by delivering on key Manifesto pledges.

Chapter Twelve – A Fairer Westminster

In the 1972 film 'The Candidate', Robert Redford pulls his campaign manager into a side room when he is unexpectedly elected to the US Senate and asks, in the last line of the film, "so what do we do now?" It wasn't quite like that fifty years later in our real-life version of winning against the odds.

Was it 'hitting the ground running' or being 'thrown in at the deep end'? Whatever the right phrase, we moved quickly and decisively. In our first 100 days we chalked up a string of achievements. By mid-August 2021, we could announce a range of cost-of-living initiatives:

- A £130,000 investment to support food banks across Westminster is at the centre of a £5.6m package of further measures designed to tackle the cost-of-living crisis.
- £340,000 invested in holiday activities and food support for low-income families
- Ahead of the return to school in September, help to 850 pupils with the cost of school uniforms.
- 50,000 council tax rebates issued and extra staff employed at Citizen's Advice Westminster to cope with the surge in questions from anxious residents.

Badged 'Fairer Westminster', our 100 first day 'check list' included,

- Plans to build more new affordable homes in Westminster, including major developments at Ebury Bridge and Church Street
- Pausing the sale of council housing and commissioning an urgent review into the previous administration's policy

- Identifying more than 100 rubbish dumping 'hot spots' where local Waste Action Squads will take targeted action
- Reinstating the previously removed second weekly waste collection for everyone who needs it
- Installing 500 new electric vehicle charging points over the coming months
- Rolling out new cycling routes, speeding up the installation of cycle hangers, working with local cycling groups and TfL
- Tackling the problems caused by dockless hire e-bikes being abandoned on our streets
- Expanding the pop-up business scheme to allow local traders to have a shop front on Oxford Street
- Action against rip-off American candy stores on Oxford Street which are fleecing customers
- Celebrating with our communities with events to mark Windrush Day, Pride and the Jubilee weekend
- Launching a new Future of Westminster Commission drawing on external experts to ensure all of Westminster gets the long-term opportunities and benefits of living in the heart of the capital.

Behind all these announcements lay a huge amount of hard work from Council officers. We had not thought what kind of reception we might get from the Council's Officers prior to the election as we did not expect to win. But we were surprised and delighted with the warm and positive response from the Council's professional staff, at all levels. The story about the two Councill officers having withdrawn their early retirement following our unexpected victory might not have been true, but it felt like it was.

In the first few days, Max Sullivan and I went to discuss Communications with Pedro Wrobel, Executive Director and Robin Campbell, Acting Director of Communications. We asked them to change the 'tone' of the Council's Communications from one which claimed the Council to be the best in Britain at everything it did, to a Council that listens to residents' concerns, that values residents' views and where consultation with residents comes first. We banned the use of the words 'world-beating' and 'world class'. Pedro and Robin understood what needed to be done and the Council's social media and other communications output changed overnight, something that was quickly noticed.

We were also fully aware that we needed some expert advice on how best to implement our ambitious Manifesto, which contained over 350 separate pledges. Over the 40 years I had been involved in writing local election Manifestos, they had rarely been read by anyone other than the political obsessives. This time, the Labour Manifesto was downloaded from the Labour Group website over 3,000 times in the week after the election. If we had published the Manifesto commercially it might have hit the "Best Sellers' list.

For this important advisory role, we turned to Neale Coleman to lead the 'Future of Westminster Commission'. Neale had a formidable record in London public services having worked for both Ken Livingstone and Boris Johnson at the Greater London Authority from 2000 to 2015. One of his main responsibilities was leading on London's Olympic bid, and the delivery of the Games and their regeneration legacy. In addition, Neale led the first Mayor's approach to housing, regeneration, health and devolution and steered multi agency groups on some of London's biggest regeneration areas. Crucially, Neale had extensive knowledge and experience of how to deliver complex development and regeneration projects.

Neale also knew Westminster well as a Maida Vale Labour Councillor from 1982-1990 and, as Deputy Leader of the Labour Group and Labour's Housing spokesperson, he played a leading role in exposing the 'Homes for Votes' scandal.

The 'Future of Westminster Commission's' job was to advise the Council on areas of policy that were critical to the future success of the City and to bring in new suggestions and perspectives. The Commission was not a decision-making body. The Commission had four 'work streams', each with its own remit and group of expert advisers.

- Housing - *Advise on increasing genuinely affordable housing. As a priority, its task was to look at options for improving the Council's response to homelessness and housing need as well as the quality of services provided to tenants and leaseholders.*
- Energy and green transition - *Advise on ways to enhance and accelerate climate action to achieve a net zero Westminster by 2040.*
- Fairness and equality - *Advise on approaches and initiatives that will enable and deliver a fairer, more equal and inclusive city.*
- Economy and employment - *Advise on how the Council enables more Westminster residents to share in the economic successes of the city.*

Each 'work stream' had a convener. Another former Westminster resident, Steve Hilditch was asked to chair the Housing 'work stream'. Steve's 50-year career in housing started as a community worker on Westminster estates in 1972. He was Head of Policy for Shelter and assistant director of housing for a London borough before becoming a housing consultant working for a wide range of councils and third sector organisations. He also worked on the London Plan, drafted the first London mayor's statutory housing strategy, and worked on the national reform of housing finance. In addition, he advised several Parliamentary Select Committees on homelessness and housing investment and he chaired the government working party that established the National Tenant Voice in 2009.

Syed Ahmed chaired the energy and green transition 'work stream'. In 2012 Syed established Energy for London, a research and campaigning organisation supporting London's progress to becoming a low-carbon city. Five years later, in 2017 he helped establish Community Energy London, which he Chairs, and was appointed by the Mayor of London as a Commissioner of the London Sustainable Development Commission.

Westminster North MP Karen Buck chaired the fairness and equality 'work stream'. Currently Shadow Minister for Social Security, she had held a number of other jobs in Government and in Opposition. She Chairs of the All-Party Parliamentary Group on Legal Aid, is co-chair of the APPG for Street Children and Vice Chair of the APPG for the Private Rented Sector.

Finally, Claudette Forbes was appointed chair of the economy and employment 'work stream'. A highly experienced economic development and regeneration professional, she had been involved at a senior level in London's development for more than 30 years and was a Non-Executive Director for the Future of London and the Connected Places Catapult.

The 'Future of Westminster Commission' quickly got to work, with regular public sessions, explaining their approach, answering questions and hearing comments from residents. Their job was not to produce glossy reports that were never read nor acted upon. The job was to deliver practical results. As part of the Commission's work, Neale Coleman enlisted the pro-bono assistance of Bloomberg Associates whose global experience helped to identify the key actions that would start the transformation process.

The culmination of the Commission's early work was the establishment of a 'North Paddington Programme', targeting action in the Harrow Road, Queen's Park and Westbourne Wards in the North Paddington area. These Wards are among the most disadvantaged in Westminster, facing significant income and health inequalities compared to neighbouring wards within Westminster, alongside crime and anti-social behaviour challenges.

The Harrow Road, Westbourne and Queen's Park Wards cover primarily residential areas, characterised by higher proportions of private and socially rented housing than other parts of Westminster. The life expectancy gap between the north-west parts of the borough and more prosperous areas of Westminster is highlighted by the 14-year gap in male life expectancy between these three wards and the Marylebone Ward. The Council had been aware of these huge disparities for many years and had even drawn up plans to tackle these deep-seated problems. However, despite drawing up plans, they had all remained on the shelf, unfunded and unimplemented. Unsurprisingly, this had led to considerable resident disenchantment with the Council and its 'promises' to regenerate the area.

The Future of Westminster Commission's work helped to focus attention on the issues and the strategies needed to address them. Importantly, the Commission identified the need for the Council to find a different way of working in the area to regain the trust and confidence of the local community. To achieve this, the North Paddington Programme was given a governance model which provided clear lines of accountability for key projects and performance. There also a strong emphasis on collaborative, 'joined-up' working between Council services and regular dialogue between the Council and the community.

Early indications were that community leaders had responded positively to this practical and collaborative process. In particular, the new way of working identified some immediate actions and changes to services which produced results for local residents, for example, the reopening of the Maida Hill toilets, regular pavement jet-washing and the planned relocation of the seating at Maida Hill Piazza. Further action to address local ASB enforcement and laying the groundwork for wider community engagement in the programme, was also identified.

To give the North Paddington Programme the means to do the job, an additional £5 million capital funding a year was allocated at the Cabinet meeting in February 2023, together with an annual revenue budget of £750,000. Overall, the aim of the programme was, *"To reduce the socio-economic and health inequalities within the borough, by improving the outcomes and opportunities for those across the north-west of Westminster, so these communities feel safer, wealthier and healthier."* Two key outcomes were identified; first, *"Reducing deprivation in the North Paddington area (measured by the indices of multiple deprivation)"* and second, *"Reducing the life expectancy gap across the borough."*

This was what 'Fairer Westminster' was all about and we had nailed our colours to the mast with a very ambitious aim. Having set out our stall, the big task now was to deliver.

****

Our top priority was to increase the number of genuinely affordable Council houses. The scale of the housing crisis was terrifying. The Council housing waiting list had more than 4,000 households registered for council housing and there were over 2,600 families living temporary accommodation, many a long way away from Westminster. By October 2022, we were able to announce

- A commitment to increase delivery of the number of genuinely affordable homes by 160 to at least 1,362 Council homes for social rent
- 84 homes previously planned for private sale in regeneration schemes at 300 Harrow Road and at Westmead in Westbourne Park would now be Council homes
- Giving priority to the delivery of Council homes on the Council's own development by shifting the previous administration's 60:40% split in favour of intermediate

rent housing to a 70:30% split in favour of council homes

- A commitment to further increase the Council's affordable housing offer through other major regeneration projects in the pipeline still to come, such as Ebury Bridge and Church Street

A huge amount of work went into the new social housing programme by Council officers, Cabinet Members and 'The Future of Westminster Commission' members. The previous programme was reviewed carefully and pragmatically scheme by scheme to determine the best approach to each project within the available resources. This was a significant first step towards meeting the council's intention to obtain as many extra homes for social rent as possible as quickly as possible. We were determined that each new Council home delivered would provide a secure, stable, and affordable solution for a Westminster family in housing need, giving them a solid foundation for a successful life in the city.

We were also working closely with the Mayor of London and secured significant additional GLA support and were able to increase the number of property acquisitions from the GLA's right to buy back fund. This enabled us to buy back former Council homes in Westminster and let them as temporary accommodation, rather than house homeless families many miles away in private accommodation. One of our immediate actions was to stop the Conservatives' previous practice of selling off 'surplus' Council property on the open market, usually flats in street properties. These were properties we could refurbish and offer to those in housing need.

Announcing this major housing initiative, Councillor Matt Noble, Cabinet Member for Climate Action, Regeneration and Renters at Westminster City Council said, *"We really care about building truly affordable, family-sized homes which meet the needs of our residents and so we can build a fairer city for everyone. The wait for a family-sized social rent home in Westminster, and across London as a whole, is massive and this new commitment to deliver truly affordable homes, which sees an emphasis on council housing for social rent in the heart of the city, is the first step in a longer pipeline of work to deliver high-quality, family homes for our local people."*

In January 2023, we were able to announce the result of the residents' ballot on the regeneration plans for Church Street sites A, B and C. The previous administration had refused to hold a residents' ballot. Not only did this deny residents a say in the future of their area, but it also meant that GLA money to increase the amount of affordable housing would not be forthcoming without a ballot. A total of 73% of voting residents living in sites A, B and C voted in favour of the proposals to re-provide all existing 228 council homes and deliver at least 156 new council homes at social rent levels, create new jobs and training opportunities as well as new shops and community facilities. With a voter turnout of 56% which included residents who had moved off the estate but have the 'right to return', the positive result meant the Council was now able to move forward with the plans, as well as unlocking funding from the Greater London Authority.

Matt Noble said, *"We're pleased that the majority of residents voted in favour of our Church Street proposals and we're committed to working with them on co-designing the scheme's B & C sites. We're serious about giving local communities more say on the future of their area and we're glad residents feel the same. This positive result will allow us to build even more social and lower rent homes needed for families in our city so we can create a fairer Westminster for everyone."*

The Council also held a residents' ballot for the Ebury Bridge regeneration scheme in January 2023. That ballot was even more emphatic, with 91% of those who voted supporting the Council's revised regeneration plans. With a 67% voter turnout, there was little doubt that our plans to deliver more Council housing from the Council's own developments was popular with Council tenants. The Ebury Bridge ballot success meant that the project now qualified for £41 million of funding from the Greater London Authority and would deliver another 130 social rent homes on top of those in the original plans.

Not only had we implemented our Manifesto commitment, but our approach to arranging ballots had been vindicated. Holding residents' ballots on both these major regeneration schemes enabled the Council to access GLA funding to deliver over 320 additional new Council homes for social rent (at least 150 at Church Street and 171 at Ebury Bridge).

These initiatives were followed in February 2023 with an announcement by the Council to invest £85 million to buy 270 homes for use as temporary housing in and around Westminster. The previous administration's 'default position' was to look to other London boroughs for temporary housing which, in turn, creates problems in those boroughs, as well as breaking family and community links for those families having to move many miles away. As Labour Leader Adam Hug said, *"For years in opposition, we were calling on the council to invest in temporary accommodation stock. We have a real problem with families being sent to the outer reaches of London instead of being able to remain in Westminster."* We were now starting the long and difficult process of reversing that previous policy.

Another issue on which we took action was on empty homes in the private sector. Our information showed that 1,150 properties registered for Council Tax in Westminster in 2022 were empty homes, a 123% rise on the previous year, with the problem most acute in Knightsbridge and Belgravia. We decided to appoint an Empty Homes Officer and set up a dedicated hotline to enable residents to report long term empty homes in Westminster.

With escalating additional Council Tax payments for the owners of long-term empty properties, we wanted to encourage more owners to let the empty homes out themselves or through housing associations or the Council. Long term empty residential properties in Westminster that have been left empty for more than 2 years currently attract a Council Tax premium of 100%, with owners of empty homes for more than 5 years paying four times the standard rate, rising to six times more for over 10 years.

As Adam Hug said, *"For many the thought of so many homes in Westminster sitting empty, essentially left to rot, while thousands wait for housing, will be hard to swallow. These measures are an important first step in tackling the issue of empty houses in Westminster, where absentee international investment can hollow out our communities and waste a vital supply of homes."*

****

Another key priority for us was to increase Council help for Westminster's most vulnerable families at a time when so many were struggling with the cost-of-living crisis. Council officers had estimated that around a quarter of households across Westminster (approximately 31,000 households) are particularly vulnerable to rises in living costs, with some people facing extreme hardship.

In June, Deputy Leader Tim Roca announced that the Council would be providing Free School Meal (FSM) vouchers to all eligible children over the six-week summer school holiday. The funding will be distributed to eligible families in the form of supermarket vouchers and equates to £15 per child per week. Tim also announced that the council will also be supporting the summer Holiday Activity and Food (HAF) programme. This enables young people aged 4 to 16 on Free School Meals to take part in free activities run by local organisations across the borough. This includes physical activities, for example, cricket, basketball and swimming, creative activities such as music and drama and days out ranging from visiting an exhibition to getting out in nature. Each child who attends an activity will receive a free meal.

In addition, for the first time, the Council made an additional £240,000 available to widen the HAF offer and reach even more young people in Westminster. This enabled young people aged up to 25, as well as those who fall just short of eligibility but are experiencing hardship, to access the activities and food during the summer holidays for free. Working with over 70 local organisations, the Council was able to
deliver sessions for children and young people in Westminster, including those with special educational needs and disabilities.

A month later, in July, Tim Roca announced that £85,000 would be invested to help families with the cost of school uniforms, as part of a package of measures to help Westminster residents struggling with rising prices. The School Uniform Support Scheme was aimed at helping Westminster resident families of children in Reception Year of a Westminster primary school from September 2022 and those Year Six pupils in Westminster primary schools that have now moved onto secondary school from September 2022 and are in receipt of Free School Meals.

Schools received £31 for every eligible child starting in Reception to help with the costs of primary school uniform. To help with the cost of secondary school uniforms, primary schools were allocated £150 for every eligible Year Six child. The new fund was in addition to existing support available to disadvantaged families via schools and the Council's Early Help services. Parents were also able to receive financial help from charities supporting young people, such as John Lyons Charity and the Portal Trust.

Further support for young people and families over the Christmas holidays was announced in December. The Council again provided Free School Meal vouchers to all eligible children in the form of supermarket vouchers. In recognition of the rising cost of food, the Council increased the value of each voucher to £17.50 per child per week, up from £15. The

Council also supported the Winter Holiday Activity and Food programme, funded by the Department for Education.

And to round off a year of intense activity on the cost-of-living front, in December the Council announced that all children attending state-funded primary schools in
Westminster would receive a free school lunch. This would save families up to £550 per child, per year. Starting in January 2023, all Key Stage 2 children (Years 3 – 6) who attend a Westminster primary school would receive a free school lunch. The money was given directly to schools and the programme would run for an initial period of 18 months.

In all, our cost-of-living support programme to help struggling families during a time of high food prices and soaring energy bills totalled more than £10 million. We were delighted to get the endorsement of health professionals for the Free School Meals programme. Dr Regina Keith, Senior Lecturer in Global Public Health & Nutrition, University of Westminster, said, *"Research indicates that universal free school meals can lead to increased willingness to learn and increased aspiration for future careers, especially for children from low-income families. With challenges facing millions of families, it is a beacon of hope to learn that Westminster City Council has selected to use their limited resources to invest in the future of their children by providing free school lunches for all primary school children.*

Local headteachers were also very supportive, with Cory Mclauchlan, Head of School at Robinsfield George Eliot Federation in St John's Wood, saying, *"Some of our most vulnerable families are really struggling this winter and there's a real danger that many families could have to choose between heating and eating. At George Eliot Primary School we have a strong commitment to providing healthy meals every day and making sure our children are always ready to learn. The free lunch offer from Westminster Council will therefore make a huge difference to families and guarantee that no child is left behind."*

This initiative made the national news. Just after Christmas, Nick Robinson on the BBC 4 Radio 'Today' programme interviewed celebrity chef Jamie Oliver at a Westminster primary school in Paddington. Jamie Oliver, a well-known supporter of healthy eating in schools, commented *"I'm proud of what they're doing here. And when you see it working . . . you do realise it's not rocket science."* I felt a warm glow and it almost brought a tear to my eye. I, too, was so proud of what we had been able to do in power. It was at that moment that I decided I had to write an account of our victorious campaign and the subsequent changes for the better we were able to bring about.

And at the Council meeting on 8th March we were able to announce that we could go further and provide free school meals to nursery, primary and secondary school children up to the age of 14. This followed the Mayor of London's decision to provide all primary school children in London with free lunches from September 2023 for one year. By using the money we had already earmarked for primary school lunches we were now able to extend the programme to include nursery children and those secondary school pupils in years 7, 8 and 9 who go to state schools and live in Westminster, at a total cost of £2 million. Adam Hug told the Council meeting, *"I want Westminster to be a place where children can sit down together in the canteen without the anxiety and stigma of who can afford to eat. That lunch may now be free for those children, but we think the impact it can have on their wellbeing and life chances could be priceless."*

****

In my area of City Management and Air Quality, we got to work very quickly. Despite having two key vacant posts – the Director of City Highways and the Director of Public Protection – the sterling efforts of senior officers Phil Robson, Jon Rowing and Nicky Crouch, who were all 'acting up', meant we could get things done.

Our first initiative was to increase the jet washing of key streets across Westminster from an annual clean to a jet wash every quarter. This made an immediate difference to the look and feel of many high streets outside the West End and demonstrated beyond doubt that we could 'get things done'. We followed this by reopening the long-closed public toilets on Carnaby Street in the West End and Maida Hill in North Paddington. Often it is the small things that make the difference and it was a lesson I was keen to follow elsewhere.

We then set up the 'Waste Action Squad' targeting regular dumping at over 100 'hot spots' across Westminster. As part of the initiative, Veolia 'deep cleaned' 50 dumping hotspots and City Inspectors carried out 209 waste interventions, including with businesses to ensure they had the right waste disposal contracts in place.

Part of the job of the 'Waste Action Squad' was to engage with residents to provide insight into local street cleanliness issues and how best to tackle them. The 'Waste Action Squad' was warmly welcomed by the 1,700 residents who the team spoke to in the first 10 months, signalling to residents that tackling on-street dumping was a priority for the Council. The Waste Action Squad didn't just talk to people it took action wherever necessary, with nearly 2,000 enforcement actions against residential waste dumping in 2022/23.

We also started a trial with CCTV cameras located in three dumping 'hot spot' areas - Denbigh Street junction in Pimlico, Foley Street in Fitzrovia and Warlock Road junction in north Paddington. Cameras were installed at these locations, which then sent footage to the viewing platform using Artificial Intelligence to identify suspected fly tippers. City Inspectors then reviewed the footage and where a vehicle is identified as being involved in a fly tipping incident, the registered vehicle keeper details were requested from the DVLA. Once an alleged offender was identified, formal enforcement action commenced either by way of an interview under caution or by the issuing of a penalty notice. If this trial is successful, we intend to extend it across other 'hot spots' and continue to take strong action against the rubbish dumpers.

We also started to take coordinated action in Queensway and Edgware Road, two of our 'high streets' which were the subject of a range of issues, including rubbish dumping, crime and anti-social behaviour, licensing and late-night disturbance. We set up 'Strategy Groups' comprising, Ward Councillors, Council Officers, major landowners and businesses, local groups and the police, to discuss the issues and plan a programme of action. I was delighted when John Zamit, Chairman of local amenity group SEBRA, wrote to me in March 2023 to say, *"huge improvement in rough sleepers situation in Queensway along with other improvements, such as hot washing of the pavements and over ten new traditional shop fronts gone in between Bayswater Road and Porchester Gardens and, as a result, six downmarket souvenir shops have subsequently closed."*

Boosting our activity on cycling was also a priority and I was fortunate to have Max Sullivan as my Deputy and as the Council's 'Cycling Champion'. Together, we made a point of meeting Will Norman, the Mayor's Walking and Cycling Commissioner, at an early stage to rebuild relations between the Council and Transport for London. The previous administration had dragged its heels on cycling issues, but we wanted to move as quickly as possible to increase safety for cyclists and to increase the number of secure cycle hangars in Westminster's residential areas.

One cycling issue that we did not anticipate was the 'explosion' in the number of e-bikes that started to flood into Westminster in the summer. There were no regulations governing the use of e-bikes, resulting in many bikes being left by their riders in dangerous locations, often obstructing the pavement. Residents, visitors and shoppers were unsurprisingly angry at having to negotiate past the e-bike hazards. We reckoned at one point, there were about 3,000 e-bikes a day parked on Westminster streets, mostly in safe places, but many which were not, creating a significant safety risk, particularly for disabled and elderly residents or visitors.

So, I instructed officers to remove and seize any bikes which were causing dangerous obstructions to pavements and roads. *"Trying to walk down some of our streets has become like attempting an obstacle course and we are fed up finding these bikes dumped across the city,"* I told the press. *"We've contacted the major e-bike operators and made it clear that if they don't remove their bikes from the pavement the council will - and we'll charge them for doing so."*

At the same as we were taking this action, we wanted to find a solution that worked for everyone and were also talking to the e-bike companies about a long-term way to provide designated parking bays for e-bikes that could be managed effectively so that e-bikes were no longer the hazard for pedestrians they currently were.

It wasn't just e-bikes that were flocking to Westminster. The Queen's Platinum Jubilee, the fine weather and, sadly, the Queen's Funeral all brought hundreds of thousands of additional visitors to Westminster and created more work for our street cleaning and waste collection teams at Veolia. In particular, our street cleaners worked around the clock during the preparations for the funeral of The Queen and kept the city clean whilst hundreds of thousands of visitors paid their respects.

We were briefed on 'Operation London Bridge', the 'code name' for the funeral arrangements, during the summer and I joked that we would be here again in four years' time as the Queen approached her 100th birthday. Sadly, it was not to be. In September, the Council undertook a huge operation to ensure that the areas around Buckingham Palace, Whitehall, the Palace of Westminster and Westminster Abbey were looking their best as Heads of State, Prime Ministers, Royalty, and members of the public arrived in central London for the funeral. In the days before the funeral, 35 additional street cleaning staff were deployed each day to provide additional cleansing around The Strand, Hyde Park, Marble Arch, Park Lane, Vauxhall Bridge Road, Marylebone, and Mayfair. The team also were responsible for sanding the route ahead of the funeral procession.

Once the Funeral Service had ended and attendees departed Westminster Abbey, Council teams got straight to work on the clean-up operation. In all, over 150 people and 19 different vehicles split across 11 separate teams helped clear litter and remove sand in readiness for the roads reopening. The clean-up operation started at 14:45pm and was completed by 17:00pm. This was quite an achievement. Thanks to our terrific Council and Veolia staff we were able to 'pass' this important test. As I commented to the press, *"When the eyes of the world were on Westminster, they truly did Her Majesty and the country proud."* And in February 2023, we were delighted when Veolia were awarded the 'Team of the Year' accolade from the 'Keep Britain Tidy' group for their work during the Funeral period.

Our Climate Emergency work was led by Councillors Matt Noble and Ryan Jude, who quickly grasped the nettle to commission an 'environmental inequalities' map. Council officers had developed a new mapping tool to show that families living in some of the more deprived communities in Westminster faced the largest number of environmental risks. The interactive Environmental Justice map used 10 environmental indicators, including air quality, building standards, proximity to green spaces and flood risk. This data was then combined with existing information about social, economic, educational and health outcomes.

The new map has helped the Council to help identify priority areas for environmental improvements, from retrofitting inefficient buildings to informing air quality monitoring and green space improvements. As Ryan Jude, Deputy Cabinet Member for Climate Action and Biodiversity said, *"This measure is an important breakthrough. Mapping and highlighting these risks gives us a better understanding of the problem so we can direct support towards communities most in need."*

More immediately, in October, the Council banned the harmful weedkiller, glyphosate, on all managed outdoor space. Glyphosate is a toxic substance in many commercial weedkillers and sprays. It has a significant environmental impact as it removes the habitats and food sources of a variety of native insects, contaminates water sources, and sustained exposure causes significant harm to key species, such as bees, that support our ecosystems. The ban incorporated all products containing glyphosate on all Council-managed outdoor spaces and housing estates. We hoped this would also encourage all landowners in Westminster to follow suit.

And on 13th March 2023, the Council, in partnership with ethical crowdfunding platform Abundance Investment, launched Westminster Green Investment, giving residents a chance to invest in sustainable projects and green initiatives within the local community to support the council's Fairer Environment target of becoming a net zero Council by 2030 and a net zero city by 2040. Aiming to raise up to £1 million in the first round, residents and businesses were able to invest from as little as £5 and earn returns of 4.2% interest a year, across five years. The money raised would help fund a range of energy efficiency measures for Council-owned buildings or community-owned sites, such as schools and community centres. We reached the £1 million target in just 9 days.

Deputy Leader Aicha Less's portfolio of Public Protection, Licensing and Communities was also quickly off the mark to tackle the long-standing scourge of pedicabs which tour the West End, charging extortionate fares to unsuspecting tourists, all while playing excessively loud music late in to the night and early morning. In July, six pedicab operators were fined over £5,000 following enforcement action by the Council, in partnership with Metropolitan Police, at City of London Magistrates Court under the Control of Pollution Act, 1974. In this round of prosecutions, fines, costs, and victim surcharges ranged between £350-£1514 for the six pedicab drivers, with a total of £5,029 being imposed.

Aicha's 'get tough' approach resulted in over 50 pedicab drivers reported for prosecutions. The council's City Inspectors, alongside the police, also moved hundreds of pedicab drivers on for creating serious accessibility issues by blocking the pavements in the busy areas of such as Covent Garden, Soho, Leicester Square, Chinatown, and Mayfair. During these operations, many riders were moved on after blocking footpaths outside theatres in Covent Garden and Leicester Square. We were looking forward to a long-promised Transport Bill to bring forward new regulations requiring pedicabs and e-bikes to be licensed. Council Leader Adam Hug, said:

"Unlicensed pedicabs are a dangerous nuisance across the West End. We've had enough of drivers blocking pavements and causing accessibility issues, annoying residents and businesses late at night, and charging extortionate fares to visitors. People visiting the West End deserve to be able to travel through our city safely without being ripped off by unregulated drivers. We will continue to work with the police to crack down on any pedicab drivers who flout the law."

Disappointingly, in January 2023, the Government announced that the promised Transport Bill had been delayed with no indication of when it might be rescheduled.

Getting tough was not confined only to pedicab operators. In December, Aicha launched the novel 'Don't Pee Off Soho' campaign against people who urinate in public. The Council started to treat walls in Soho with a 'pee paint' that give perpetrators a nasty surprise if they attempt to relieve themselves on it. The paint created a water-repellent layer so that urine and other liquid bounce back onto the perpetrator doing the peeing, leaving them covered in their own urine.

There may have been a humorous angle to the campaign, but the issue was deadly serious, particularly for West End residents. Incidents of public urination in central London had increased significantly since Covid-19 restrictions were lifted and the constant smell of urine in side streets was extremely unpleasant. On top of that, cleaning up the urine was costing the Council nearly £950,000 a year. Measures to tackle the problem also included handing out penalty fines to those 'caught in the act'. Hospitality businesses were offered posters for their premises, urging people to go before they left the venue. As Aicha said, *"It's finally pee-back time and we're taking action to stop people using alleyways or doorways as a toilet. I encourage visitors to go before you leave the venue or use the public toilets around Soho and Westminster instead of using alleyways or side streets."*

****

Sorting out the Oxford Street situation was another major task, not least after we found out that the previous administration had spent about £35 million with precious little show for it beyond some glossy plans and 'strategies'. We wanted to get 'under the skin' of the Oxford Street District programme to work what had gone so badly wrong, so that we didn't fall into similar traps and to put everything right that had gone wrong. At the same time, we wanted a positive working relationship with senior staff and had no intention of embarking on a 'witch hunt'. After the traumas of the Marble Arch Mound fiasco, the last thing the organisation needed was to be 'put through the mill' in public again.

In October, Stuart Love, the City Council's Chief Executive, commissioned Mike Cooke, former Chief Executive of the London Borough of Camden, to undertake an independent review to learn any lessons from the Oxford Street District programme. Mike Cooke was asked to make any recommendations as to how we could continue to improve our processes. The terms of reference for the independent review were:

"Undertake an independent review of the Oxford Street District project commencing from 2018 through to the current date. The review to focus on the following areas:

- *The process and governance in place as well as to make recommendations on any changes or improvements that could be made for the future*
- *Review the spend on the project to date and the outputs achieved.*
- *Assist in recommending any lessons to be learnt, including for existing and future projects.*
- *In considering the lessons to be learnt from the Oxford Street District programme, consider whether the reforms undertaken following the Marble Arch Mound review are sufficient and robust enough.*
- *The review to be undertaken by an independent person. The independent person will have access to all necessary Council staff and documentation.*
- *The Chief Executive will commission the review with the outcomes being reported directly to the Leader of the Council and the Cabinet. The final report may also be considered by the relevant Scrutiny Committee of the Council. It is intended the findings of the review are published, subject to any commercial or other confidentiality issues."*

In February 2023, Mike Cooke's Independent Review revealed that up until July 2022, the Oxford Street District project had spent £34 million, comprising:

- £16 million on work which delivered just two of the 32 proposed schemes in the OSD programme: the Photography Quarter and temporary pavement widening on Oxford Street West.

- £8bmillion on contractual operating costs (overheads) billed by the prime contractor, including £80,000 per month on renting an unnecessary office throughout the pandemic.
- £6 million on the Marble Arch Mound.
- £4 million on design and preparatory works for future projects.

The Independent Review criticised the previous administration for its poor financial controls which meant that *"identifying the allocation of the costs between the various elements of the programme has proved to be very challenging for officers."* The Independent Review also endorsed the Council's new approach, stating that *"this refresh and refocusing appears to be being effective (including in reducing the programme overhead costs) and in my view appears to be an appropriate response."* We were pleased that the Independent Review had been completed in time for the Council's Budget meeting on 8th March.

Just as important as understanding the reasons why the previous Oxford Street plans had failed, we wanted to make quick progress on getting Oxford Street back on its feet. The situation was dire, as the *'Financial Times'* described:

"Stretching just over a mile east from Marble Arch, London's Oxford Street has long been one of the city's premier shopping destinations. It remains one of Europe's busiest shopping streets and, as recently as 2018, could command rents of more than £1,000 per square foot, among the most expensive in Europe. But since the onset of the Covid-19 pandemic, Oxford Street has become barely recognisable. Footfall has declined almost 60 per cent compared with 2019, according to a study by Mytraffic and Cushman & Wakefield. New commercial buildings — comprising tens of thousands of square feet of empty retail space — alternate with tatty souvenir stores and shuttered storefronts."

Led by Councillor Geoff Barraclough, we took a detailed look at the situation and early on we decided to take a more focused approach to delivering improvements for Oxford Street. We were also very conscious of the imminent arrival of the full opening of the Elizabeth Line which would increase footfall in Oxford Street considerably, bringing pedestrian safety to the forefront.

Rather spread our attention across a much wider area, we decided to prioritise reviving Oxford Street itself and a small number of adjacent areas with a combination of Council and private sector funding. At the heart of our plans were wider pavements, more seating, additional greening an enhanced lighting, as well as the encouragement of a more diverse set of activities including leisure and culture. Alongside the public realm improvements, we also pledged to work with landowners to encourage innovative use of underused retail spaces and to continue the successful 'pop-up' programme.

We were also determined to listen to local stakeholders regularly so that we could embark on this major project in partnership with the community. We set up a new governance approach, including an Oxford Street Advisory Board comprising local residents' groups and amenity societies from Soho, Mayfair, Fitzrovia and Marylebone and local businesses.

An immediate issue was dealing with the proliferation of 'American candy stores' which had spread along Oxford Street. Councillor Adam Hug told the *'Financial Times'*, "The rash of mixed sweet and souvenir shops which sprung up on Oxford Street during lockdown have by general consent dragged the tone of the area down as well as in some cases opening flouting trading standards laws. They have fleeced both customers and the taxpayer through widespread evasion of business rates amounting to around £8m."

We reckoned some of the properties were used to avoid business rate bills and possibly commit other offences, including selling counterfeit and unsafe goods. As the *'Financial Times'* explained, *"the identities of the ultimate occupiers were increasingly hard to track, often hidden in a web of subtenants, agents, intermediaries and shell companies. Many of the businesses are wound up without ever having filed accounts. That has made collecting property taxes almost impossible."* This was 'big business' and we were working with the Police, HMRC and the National Crime Agency. Action by the Council in the autumn had managed to collect £250,000 in business rates arrears from sweet and souvenir shops and we were successful in reducing the number of these shops by a third, from 30 to 21, through a combination of trading standards and legal action. On one raid, the Council recovered 14,000 suspect items from just two shops on Oxford Street.

However, by February 2023, the situation had reversed, according to research by
Local Data Company (LDC), leading to Council leader Adam Hug arguing, *"We are dealing here with a sophisticated operation that is skilled at exploiting UK legal loopholes. There is a glaring lack of governance around setting up companies in the UK with only cursory checks on who the directors are – there are more checks involved if you want to get a local authority library lending card. We need the new Economic Crime Bill to help clamp down on these loopholes and to provide government agencies such as Companies House and HMRC with the powers and funding they need."*

Our concerns about London's reputation as the 'European centre for money laundering', led us to launching a "Westminster against dirty money" campaign at the Council meeting in September 2022. At the meeting we agreed a motion to sign the Fair Tax Pledge, aligning the Council with major companies and public sector organisations in the UK committed to ensuring transparency in tax. We also committed to work with others to tackle the scourge of economic crime and international corruption in the Westminster property market. We followed this on 22nd with an open forum, including major property developers, leading anti-corruption experts and representatives from key government agencies.

Council research revealed that Westminster had seen a 300% rise in the number of properties registered to owners in Jersey since 2010 and a rise of 1,200% in the number of properties registered to owners in Russia. While Westminster is home to a cosmopolitan population, the explosion in investment underlined our fears that property was being used to launder money of questionable origin.

We, therefore, called on central Government to make major changes to stop London being a soft touch for investors with dubious money to spend, including:

- Tightening UK procurement laws to restrict the artificial use of tax havens and low-tax jurisdictions
- A commitment in the forthcoming Economic Crime Bill to a proper level of resourcing for the National Crime Agency and HMRC to fight money laundering, together with tougher penalties for failing to comply with money laundering supervision requirements
- Increasing the fee to register a company at Companies House from £12 to £50 and introducing more rigorous identity checks
- Properly implementing the newly passed but long delayed beneficial ownership register of property to deliver transparency about ownership

Council Leader Adam Hug said, *"Westminster's dirty secret has been known for many years but those in power looked the other way for too long as money of questionable origin flooded into London and investors took advantage of our relatively lax laws.*

It took the war in Ukraine to refocus attention on oligarch investments and what London has become in terms of a European laundromat for dirty money. But the problem goes wider than Putin and his henchman, to many others who see Belgravia, Knightsbridge, Mayfair and other parts of Westminster as places to rinse their money. This not only damages the reputation of our city by supporting authoritarianism abroad but drains the vitality of areas with empty or under-used homes."

To coincide with the first anniversary of the invasion of Ukraine on 24th February 2023, the Council renamed a small section of Bayswater Road close to the Russian Embassy, as Kyiv Road. We were delighted when His Excellency Vadym Prystaiko, Ukraine's ambassador to the UK, welcomed this initiative, saying,

"Kyiv Road is a symbol of solidarity with the Ukrainian people and a tribute to their unwavering spirit in the face of aggression. It is a reminder that the struggle of Ukraine has the attention of the international community. We are grateful to the Westminster City Council and its residents for their support in honouring our nation's capital and its brave defenders."

A few days later, West End Ward Councillor Paul Fisher sent a message to the Labour Group, *"Went for a meal with Ukrainian friends last night and they felt it was a really poignant reminder that they're welcome and supported here in the UK."*

****

At the Council meeting on 8th March 2023, we announced the delivery of a key Manifesto pledge – a freeze in the Westminster City Council part of the Council Tax for the next year. This meant Westminster would continue to offer the cheapest Band D rate in the country. A 2% increase in social care spending sanctioned by the Government meant Westminster Band D residents would have an increase of just 18p per week.

In addition, we launched a £1 million 'Rent Support Fund' to help social housing tenants most in need of help as they faced an 7% increase from April 2023. The money would cover some or all of the rent increases for households who are not entitled to Universal Credit or Housing Benefit.

Every Cabinet Member was given a 5 minute 'slot' to highlight the key facts and figures from their portfolios. This was an opportunity for us all to show how far we had come in less than a year. My brief contribution covered the wide horizon of my responsibilities,

"Nearly one year on from the historic Labour victory and my planned retirement. I have never worked so hard. So much done. So much more to do.

City Management and Air Quality is a massive portfolio – roads, pavements, parking, cycling, walking, waste collection and recycling, trees, parks, public toilets, street lighting, bridges, cemeteries…and the mortuary. And apologies for any services I have missed out. So here are a few highlights.

Our Waste Action Squad is tackling waste and rubbish dumping throughout the City.

We have undertaken nearly 2,000 enforcement actions against residential waste, with an expected total of around 3,200 enforcement actions for the full year.

We have spoken to over 1,700 people on our streets. For the first time we are working directly with the community on waste and recycling issues, including in Soho where we are appointing an additional City Inspector focussing on commercial waste.

We have collected over 1,000 tonnes of food waste since we rolled out the recycling service.

On Active travel, we are developing more cycle routes throughout the city, such as the Cleveland Street cycle route where we are working closely with Camden.

We will be installing 60 more secure bike hangers, providing safe parking for 360 bikes, and 250 cycle stands giving 500 extra parking places. In all, over 850 additional cycle parking places will be provided across Westminster.

We are working with e-bike operators to get the e-bikes off the pavement and into dedicated bays. We are also urging the operators to raise the fines for those who continue to dump the e-bikes and cause obstruction to pedestrians.

We are working closely with the Mayor, both on delivering improved cycle routes and in expanding the Santander Cycle docking station network in north Paddington.

We are working with the hospitality industry and property and landowners to reduce PM 2.5 emissions. We are encouraging the installation of electric cooking hobs in Westminster's restaurants, bars, cafes and hotels.

And there is more

- *Westminster's high streets are now jet washed 4 times a year - up from just once a year under the previous regime*
- *800 more Electric Vehicle charging points will be installed by the end of the financial year, with a further 200 to follow*
- *The introduction of smart charging means the EV owners are saving £4 each time they charge their cars. A user charging their EV car twice a week saves £32 a month.*
- *A micro-logistics hub is open at the Cambridge Street car park in Pimlico from where 2,000 parcels a day will be delivered by cargo bikes, reducing the number of vehicles on the road*

- *Three CCTV cameras have been located at dumping hotspots in Fitzrovia, Pimlico and Paddington, taking pictures of the dumpers so that we can follow up with enforcement action*

I am certainly enjoying retirement. You know why? We are getting things done!"

We had got through our first budget, delivered a string of Manifesto pledges and we were running the Council in a professional and determined manner. No more 'Failing Better'. The pain of repeated election defeats had gone and all the 'redoubling of effort' had been worth it.

And the re-election campaign has already started. Nothing succeeds like success. Our regular email *'Action Reports'* continues to be sent to all the Labour-held and 'split 'wards. We have set up regular advice surgeries in Hyde Park, Lancaster Gate and Vincent Square Wards where previously there had been none. Regular door-to-door canvassing and newsletter delivery sessions are happening across Westminster in preparation for the next Mayoral and General Elections scheduled for 2024. The momentum generated by the Council election campaign victory has brought in new Labour members, young and old, who want to be associated with a Council that is 'getting things done'.

When some people say, *"they're all the same",* I hope that this account of what Westminster Labour was able to achieve in the first year of a Labour Council will persuade the doubters that political change can bring about real practical benefits and improvements to the lives of very many people. I am so glad that I have been able to be part of this.

Acknowledgements

I would like to thank those who helped make this book possible.

Much of the material I have used is from the very many Westminster Labour Group press releases issued during the campaign and thanks are due to Adam Hug, David Boothroyd and Geoff Barraclough for their accounts of their week-by-week activities.

I have extensively mined Andrew Murray's 'State of Soho' and Dave Hill's 'On London' blogs for their thoughts and their analysis of the electoral and demographic trends at play in the West End and wider Westminster area. Both blogs provided independent viewpoints to balance my Labour prejudice. Thanks, too, to the 'Soho Clarion' and 'SEBRA News' magazines which gave very helpful insights into the issues of importance to the Soho, Bayswater and Lancaster Gate communities.

Huge thanks to Paul Wheeler who read the first draft and identified the gaps that needed to be filled, as well as encouraging me to complete the project so that others could understand how we had achieved our success.

Thanks, too, to my sister Sharon, together with friends Janice Kok and Pamela Davenport for their very helpful comments on the draft.

Finally, the biggest thank you is to Linda, Amelia and Zoe for their love and support and without whom I would not have had the inspiration to write a single word.

Bibliography

Anthony, Andrew, *'UK local elections: how London turned from blue to red'*, The Observer, 8th May 2022

Apps, Peter, *'New Westminster Council leader interview: borough plans investment in temporary housing and more homes for social rent',* Inside Housing, 13th February 2023

Ball, Jonny, *"The Tories are seen as increasingly anti-London", says Westminster's first Labour leader",* New Statesman, 4th July 2023

Belton, Catherine, *'In British PM race, a former Russian tycoon quietly wields influence',* Reuters, 19th July 2019

Bentham, Martin, *'London elections 2022: Will Partygate help Labour snatch Westminster from Tories?',* Standard, 3rd May 2022

Brooke, Rodney, *'The Councillor: Victim or Vulgarian?'* Local Government Association, 2005

Butler, Patrick, *'Pancho Lewis: 'We refused to accept that the West End had to be Tory'*, Guardian, 17th July 2018

Clark, Dan, Harlow, Max and O'Murchu, Cynthia, *'How Oxford Street was overrun by sweet shops'*, Financial Times, 17th August 2022

Cooke, Mike, *'Independent Review of Westminster City Council's Oxford St District Programme'*, Westminster City Council, February 2023

Davies, Harry, and Harding, Luke, *'Revealed: top female Tory donor's vast offshore empire with husband'*, Guardian, 4th October 2021

Dimoldenberg, Paul, *'The Westminster Whistleblowers',* Politicos, 2006

Dimoldenberg, Paul, *'Time for change in Westminster – why we need an elected Mayor',* Westminster Labour Party, January 2020

Dimoldenberg, Paul, *'How Westminster Labour won the Tory stronghold of Hyde Park ward',* Labour List, 30th May 2022

Elgot, Jessica, *'The shaming of Whitehall: how the Partygate scandal unfolded',* Guardian. 19th May 2022

Foot, Tom, *'Marble Arch Mound: anger at 'top-down' Tories',* Westminster Extra, 20th August 2021

Foot, Tom, *'Election fairy tale for man believed to be the country's longest-serving opposition councillor',* Westminster Extra, 13th May 2022

Hill, Dave, *'Could the Conservatives lose Westminster Council?'* On London, 28th December 2017

Hill, Dave, *'Borough Elections 2022: Labour's uphill task in Tory Westminster',* On London, 28th April 2022

Hill, Dave, *'Westminster: Historic first Labour council outlines new approach',* On London, 18th May 2022

Jude, Ryan and Ormsby, Ellie, *'Winning Westminster was a historic turning of the tide. Here's how we did it',* Labour List, 4th June 2022

Lemann, Nicholas, *'Only Connect',* The New Yorker, 31st October 2022

Lewis, Pancho, *'My time as a Soho Councillor',* Soho Clarion, Spring 2022

Local Government Boundary Commission for England, *'Final recommendations published for City of Westminster'*, LGBCE, May 2020

Lord, Tim, *'The Property Connection - Property Companies and their links to Westminster City Council'*, Soho Clarion, Spring 2022

Malone, Andrew, *'Meet Dave's other chums who made billions under Putin and are bankrolling the Tories'*, Daily Mail, 25th July 2014

Marriott, Oliver, *'The Property Boom'*, Pan Piper, 1967

Marylebone Association, *'Monthly Newsletter'*, September 2021

Murray, Andrew, *'Westminster Council election results have usually been a foregone conclusion. But there are signs that the 2018 local elections could be different.'* State of Soho, 12th December 2017

Murray, Andrew, *'Decision Day!'*, State of Soho, 4th May 2022

Murray, Andrew, *'The Red Flag is flying over Westminster'*, 'Soho Clarion' Summer 2022

MVRDV, *'Learning from Marble Arch Mound: A Premature Opening and an Execution Lacking in Love (Our side of the story)'*, MVRDV, 28th January 2022

Public Health England, *'Westminster Local Authority Health Profile 2019'*, 3rd March 2020

Stratton, Harry, *'Property Developers Have No Place in Local Government'*, Jacobin, 19th January 2022

Sullivan, Conor, *'Airbnb rentals in London block sparks call for action'*, Financial Times, 7th December 2018

Sumeray, Derek, *'Track the Plaque'*, Breedon Books, 2003

Watkins. Jack, *'Paddington Station: The everyday masterpiece, still a marvel 165 years on'*, Country Life, 21st March 2021

Weaver, Matthew, *"People are just desperate': how London turned on the Tories'*, Guardian, 7th May 2022

Westminster City Council, *'Senior Salaries at Westminster Council, April 2021'*, December 2021

Westminster City Council, *'Internal Review – Marble Arch Mound Report,'* 21st October 2021

Westminster City Council, *'Westminster Libraries and Archives: Overview of Transformation and Next Steps'*, February 2022

Westminster City Council, *'Hyde Park Ward Profile'*, 2022

Westminster Labour Party, *'Labour's Plan for a Fairer Westminster'*, March 2022

About the Author

Paul Dimoldenberg was born in Manchester in 1950. He attended Bury Grammar School and studied Town Planning at the Polytechnic of Central London and Oxford Polytechnic. He worked in local government from 1975 -1988, after which he followed a career in public relations, culminating in the establishment, with colleagues, of Quatro PR in 2007 which he now chairs.

Paul was first elected to Westminster City Council for the Harrow Road Ward in May 1982 until 1990. In October 1997, he was elected for the Queen's Park Ward which he served until May 2022. In May 2022, he was elected for the Hyde Park Ward. Paul was Leader of the Labour Opposition from 1987-1990 and from 2004-2015.

He is the author of 'The Westminster Whistleblowers', the story of Dame Shirley Porter and the 'Homes for Votes' and 15p Cemeteries scandals.

In 2020, Paul wrote 'Cheer Churchill. Vote Labour: The story of the 1945 General Election', followed later that year by 'Building the New Jerusalem: How Attlee's Government built one million new homes'. In 2021, Paul wrote a life of London's Education pioneer, Sir Ashley Bramall, called "A Sense of Duty'.

Paul is married to Linda. They live in Marylebone and they have two grown-up daughters, Amelia and Zoe.